SPACE AGE

The complete Space Shuttle vehicle. The Orbiter is mounted on its External Fuel Tank, and flanked by the two Solid Rocket Boosters. Orbiter Enterprise, now being used for ground tests only, took part in May 1979 in this first roll-out from the Vehicle Assembly Building to the Cape Canaveral launchpad 5.6 km away. (Compare Shuttle size with men on Transporter)

SPACE AGE

REGINALD TURNILL

Illustrated with coloured and
black-and-white photographs
and diagrams

FREDERICK WARNE

Cover illustration: Space Projects 1980–2025 reprinted from Grumman Aerospace magazine *Horizons*. Grummans built the Lunar Module which landed men on the Moon; their future projects include the Beam Builder described in this book for constructing future space stations

ISBN 0 7232 2408 0

Typeset by CCC, printed and bound in Great Britain
by William Clowes (Beccles) Limited,
Beccles and London
1293·879

CONTENTS

ACKNOWLEDGMENTS

Many people have contributed, by their work and writings, to the information contained in SPACE AGE. First come the staff of the National Aeronautics and Space Administration (NASA) who are responsible for America's civil space programmes, and the US Defense Department, responsible for military space and 'spy satellites'. Then come the aerospace firms who work for NASA, and have their own teams of scientists and designers, beginning with Rockwell International, prime contractors for the Space Shuttle, and Grumman, Boeing, Lockheed, McDonnell Douglas, Martin Marietta, TRW, Hamilton Standard and many others. The Novosti Press Agency and the BBC Monitoring Service have provided much information about Soviet space activities to supplement that in the author's own books, *The Observer's Spaceflight Directory* and *The Observer's Book of Manned Spaceflight* (also published by Frederick Warne (Publishers) Ltd). The European Space Agency and British Aerospace have also helped with information about both their own and other organizations' projects. All of them have helped most generously with photographs. The Industrial Art Studio was responsible for some of the diagrams. Magazines consulted include America's *Aviation Week and Space Technology*, and *Air Force Magazine* and Britain's *Flight International* and *Spaceflight*. Among very many books consulted have been Professor Gerard O'Neill's *The High Frontier* (Corgi); T A Heppenheimer's *Colonies in Space* (New English Library); *Encyclopaedia of Astronomy and Space* (Macmillan), and Adrian Berry's *The Iron Sun* (Coronet). Angus Macpherson kindly read the proofs. My thanks, as always, are due to my wife, Margaret Turnill, for research, checking and typing.

Note on Abbreviations   The usual metric abbreviations, km for kilometres, m for metres, l for litres etc, have been used in this book; also t for tonnes, M for millions, B for billions. Other abbreviations are explained when they first appear in the text.

Author introducing Dr Wernher von Braun, designer of the Saturn 5 rocket, during a BBC TV interview shortly before he died. It was during this interview that he made the statement quoted below

DEDICATION

This book is dedicated to my former enemy and later friend, the man whose rockets got the Apollo astronauts to the Moon—the late Dr Wernher von Braun. Shortly before he died in 1977, he told me:

'If I were 10 or 15 years old I would very definitely commit myself and my life to the space programme. I think there are tremendous opportunities and challenges out there. I just envy the youngsters who have a chance of going on where we leave off'.

CHAPTER ONE

SPACE AGE

Section 1   A New and Exciting World, Waiting to be Explored

The Space Age promises a new and exciting world, with fresh opportunities for young people with courage and a sense of adventure to go out and explore it. This book tries to explain what some of these opportunities are, and how they have come about.

It has taken almost exactly 100 Soviet and American spacemen—supported of course by thousands of ground-based astronomers, scientists, mathematicians and engineers—to make those opportunities possible. The 12 men who have walked on the Moon found it was a place where they could work *and* have fun—the two most important things which make people different from other animals. The astronauts and cosmonauts who have been in space, and the unmanned spacecraft which in the last few years have visited five of our planets and sent back pictures and information about them, have proved that there is no need any more to think of space as a place of terror, inhabited by all sorts of hostile creatures and mysterious forces, as suggested so often in books and comics.

The fact is that our Solar System, with its nine planets and their 34 moons, is strictly neutral. So far as we know, there is no one out there likely to object when our explorers arrive; but there is no one to help them, either. Earlier explorers learned to live in the blazing heat of the Earthly deserts, and fearsome cold of the polar regions, by making suitable clothes; they got to the top of Mount Everest (only a quarter of a century ago!) by taking their own oxygen with them, because at that height there is not really enough air to breathe. There *were* hostile animals and insects in the jungles and deserts and polar regions who did object to men invading their territory.

Some people think a manned expedition to Mars is not worth considering because the men concerned will be away from Earth for at least 18 months, and probably $2\frac{1}{2}$ years. They forget that Charles Darwin,

*To reach the top of Mt Everest, Sir Edmund Hillary had to take his own 'environment'
(protective clothing and oxygen mask), just as the Apollo astronauts needed spacesuits to visit
the Moon*

the famous naturalist, was away for *five years* on the famous voyage of
exploration by HMS *Beagle* from 1831–36.

The exploration and occupation of space has so far proved less difficult,
and less dangerous, than exploring the Earth's surface. At the time of
writing, not one American astronaut has lost his life in space; the Russians
have lost only four. Measure that against the tremendous space
achievements of the last 22 years, and the fact that building a big bridge
on Earth usually costs around seven lives as a result of accidents!

Learning from the Earthly explorers and mountaineers, the early
astronauts and cosmonauts found they could live in space by wearing
spacesuits, and by taking with them the air they needed to breathe. With
the information they have brought back, enthusiastic scientists and
engineers, mostly in American and Soviet space centres, have worked out
ways of first making small space stations, say for 12 men and women, and
using them as a base for building settlements in which hundreds, and then
thousands of men and women can live *and work* very comfortably indeed.
The most astonishing thing about those settlements is that they will not be
based on the Moon or any of the planets. Although the settlements will

The nine astronauts who worked in America's Skylab space station for a total of 171 days in 1973/4 proved that men could work almost as well in space as on Earth

need material quarried from the Moon, it has been discovered that it will be much more practical to build the new settlements in space itself—man-made moons, in fact.

It is the very fact that space is neutral that is such a help. The absence of air, the fact that once placed there, there are no worries about people and houses falling down, is a help instead of a problem. On Earth the natural laws of gravity, which make hot water rise and cold water sink, are used to make central-heating systems work. In space everything is weightless and we can make use of that, too. Liquids and materials, like gold, steel and aluminium, which have very different weights on Earth, are all the same in space, where nothing has any weight at all. So huge flimsy structures which on Earth would collapse under their own weight like a pack of cards, can be assembled in space and will last almost indefinitely. It will not be necessary, for instance, to have teams of men for ever painting them to prevent them going rusty, as with our Earthly bridges.

So this book tries to show how, as men go off in steadily increasing numbers to live and work in space, they plan to create their own conditions. They will make their own climate. Just as an air-conditioned house is warmed in the winter and cooled in the summer, so that it doesn't very much matter what the weather is like outside, so *Space Age* people will control the climate of their whole space settlement. The sun will always shine, just as much or as little as they want it to. The swimming pools and lakes will always be just right—either for swimming, or for the fish that will be bred in them. The fields will get the right mixture of sun and rain to make the crops grow round the year. If a good hard frost is needed to kill diseases in the soil, that can be arranged too.

Men have always dreamed of creating a perfect world like that. Sir Thomas More invented the word 'Utopia' to describe it in a book he wrote in 1516. The problem has always been that no matter how comfortable and pleasant their world may be, men usually quarrel and fight amongst themselves, and there is the possibility that they will do that in space as well, which is also dealt with in Section 42 of this book. But much more important are the sections explaining that, for the first time in history, a whole series of 'Utopias' *can* be built by men. We know how to set about it, how to make the necessary tools, and where to get the materials to build the Utopias.

And it seems we have discovered all this just in time. There are now more than 5000 million people scratching a living—and for most of them not a very good living—on what scientists now call, not Mother Earth, but Spacecraft Earth. Unless we do something about it, Spacecraft Earth's batteries and fuel supplies are likely to run down quite soon. In the view of many of our scientists and thinkers—myself among them—people *must* get out into space, in order to find and send back to those on Earth fresh supplies of heat, energy and materials.

What is really a new Industrial Revolution has already begun. But instead of the hardships and miseries which that brought to England in the 19th Century, this one *can*—if we give it a chance—bring increased prosperity to the whole of Spacecraft Earth, including the thousands of millions who at present don't have proper homes or enough to eat. For those young people eager to take an active part in creating the Space Age it means opportunities for travel and adventure such as have not been known since the days of Elizabethan heroes like Drake and Raleigh.

Section 2 *Spaceplanes for the Space Age*

Both America and Russia are building spaceplanes. Instead of being used

Orbits of the Planets

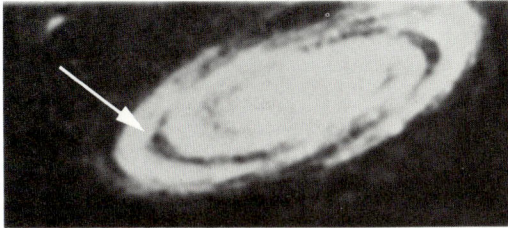

The Milky Way Galaxy (arrow shows approx. position of Solar System)

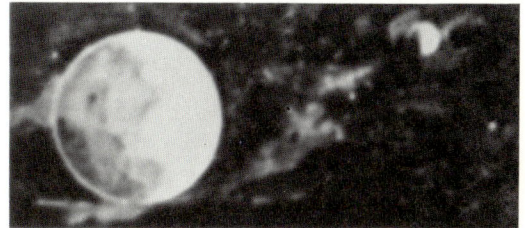

The Earth and Moon

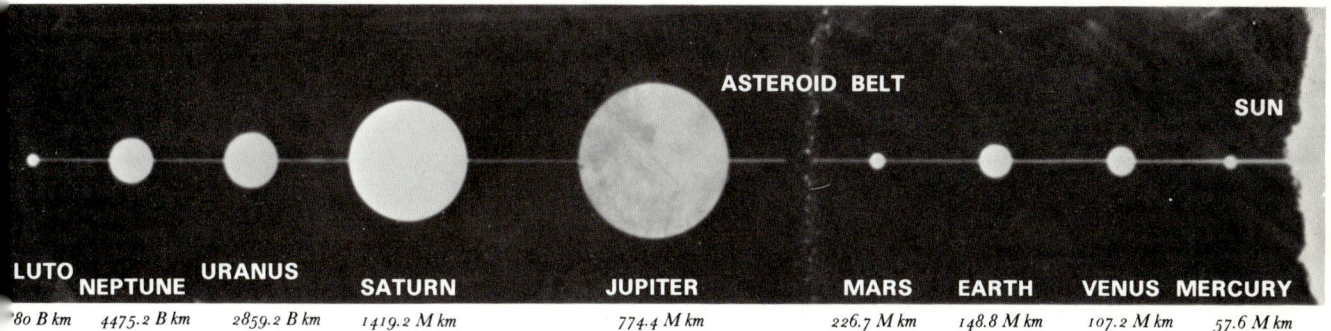

ASTEROID BELT

SUN

LUTO	NEPTUNE	URANUS	SATURN	JUPITER	MARS	EARTH	VENUS	MERCURY
80 B km	4475.2 B km	2859.2 B km	1419.2 M km	774.4 M km	226.7 M km	148.8 M km	107.2 M km	57.6 M km

Relative sizes of Planets and approximate distances from the Sun

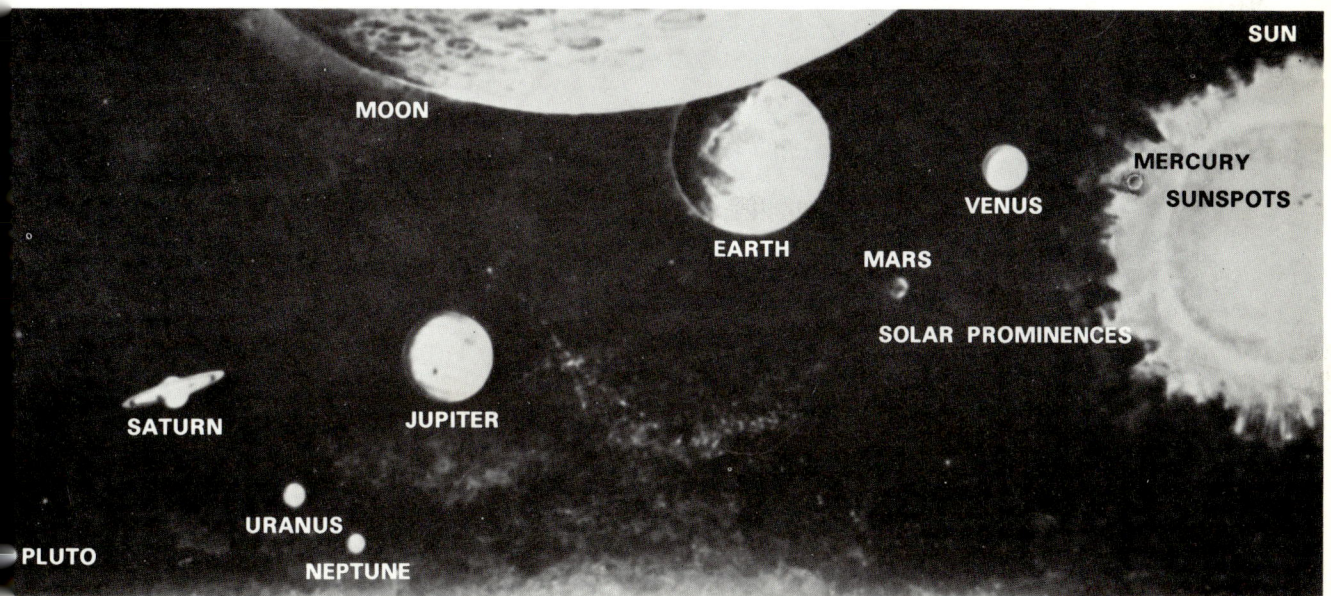

SUN

MOON

EARTH

MARS

VENUS

MERCURY

SUNSPOTS

SOLAR PROMINENCES

SATURN

JUPITER

URANUS

NEPTUNE

PLUTO

The Solar System as seen looking towards Earth from the Moon

Russia has revealed few details of the Space Shuttle she is developing, but this Soviet magazine picture may provide a clue. Though known to be smaller than America's Shuttle, it is expected that both Russia's launcher and Orbiter will be manned and recoverable

only once, like rocket-launched spacecraft, they can be used regularly for years, more like conventional jetplanes. We do not know very much as yet about Russia's spaceplane. But America's spaceplane, although it returns to Earth and lands like a glider, still has to be launched by rockets. That is because so far we have not been able to make anything except rockets powerful enough to reach the speed of 28,000 kph and a height of about 185 km which is necessary to place objects in orbit.

By the mid 1980s the United States of America expect to have a weekly service of spaceplanes. That is why they have been called Space Shuttles. They are building five to do exactly that: shuttle back and forth between Earth and orbit, carrying men and equipment.

Since the first man went into orbit in 1961—that was Yuri Gagarin, a

14

Columbia, America's first Space Shuttle, arriving 'piggyback' on Boeing 747 carrier jet at Kennedy Space Center in readiness for first orbital flight. Vertical Assembly Building in background. Later Shuttles will be named Challenger, Discovery and Atlantis. Enterprise, which made the first 'drop tests' in 1977, is being used for ground tests

Russian—we have learned to make use of space in many different ways, which are explained later in this book. Already Soviet cosmonauts have lived and worked in space continuously for 175 days in their Salyut Space Stations. However, most of the benefits affecting ordinary people on Earth have so far been brought about by unmanned spacecraft. Communications satellites bounce TV pictures around the world so that, whether you are in Australia, Japan, America or Europe, you can watch what is going on in other parts of the world as it actually happens. Weather satellites give us advance warning of storms and floods; police satellites watch oil tankers, so that quick action can be taken if by accident or on purpose they pollute the seas with their oil.

Now, instead of having to use a separate rocket for almost every satellite, the Space Shuttle can take up to five on each flight, and place them in orbit. And before returning, the Shuttle astronauts can go and repair those within reach that have broken down or need new batteries; and even bring back to Earth those which can't be repaired, so that they and their empty rocket casings won't clutter up the space above Earth, like litter in our streets.

Earth is becoming increasingly crowded, but space is unlimited; and while it may be inconvenient having to take your own oxygen with you to breathe, there are balancing advantages: once in orbit, the Space Shuttle cannot crash like an aircraft in the atmosphere, nor sink like a ship in a rough sea.

So the Shuttle will provide America with an ideal vehicle to start building the permanent space stations described in detail in Section 10. Since Russia's Shuttle is apparently smaller, and at least five years behind America's, the Russians are expected to develop their manned space stations by joining up Salyut-type modules. Because it costs so much to get started, other countries have been invited to join the American and Russian space programmes. For instance, 11 European countries, including Britain, have formed the European Space Agency, and are building Spacelab (short for 'space laboratory') for use in America's Space Shuttle.

By then, only two minutes after lift-off, the Shuttle is travelling at 5000 kph; and with much less weight to lift, it is now much easier for the Shuttle's three main engines to increase the speed. Six minutes later the speed has risen to 28,000 kph. The Shuttle is now upside down in relation to Earth, and just before it goes into orbit, the huge External Tank, now almost empty, is also jettisoned. As the Shuttle goes into orbit, 110 km high, the tank falls back into the sea. At present, these tanks cannot be recovered. Later, because they almost reach orbital speed, it is planned to send them into orbit too. They can then wait there, in 'parking orbits', for use as 'building blocks' when large space stations are being assembled.

With a final push from the two Orbit Manoeuvring System (OMS) engines, the astronauts, now weightless and safely in orbit, have time to look around and check the systems. They can roll the Shuttle, and change its attitude (in pitch, yaw and roll) by using the 44 RCS (reaction control system) engines, which can be seen as groups of holes on the nose and tail.

Then they open the Payload Bay doors, and in this picture use their remotely controlled arms to place a huge satellite in space. Because this one is to be sent into a much higher, stationary orbit at 35,680 km, it has an upper stage rocket, or Space Tug, attached to it. When the Shuttle has moved to a safe distance, the Space Tug is fired to send the satellite on its way, controlled either by the Shuttle crew, or more likely by Mission Control from Earth.

CHAPTER TWO

HOW THE SPACE SHUTTLE WORKS

Section 3   Launch Sequence

In Picture 1, the Space Shuttle is shown lifting off from its Cape Canaveral launchpad. Depending on its mission, it can stay in orbit for up to a month; but many flights will be much shorter if it is just delivering or collecting a spacecraft. It has room for up to 12 crewmen, but usually there won't be more than seven men and women aboard. For launch, the Shuttle is fixed to the External Tank, the large cylinder in the centre, which is filled with propellant—liquid oxygen and liquid hydrogen (see Section 20 on how rockets work). This is mixed together and fed into the Shuttle's three main engines. They are used only once on each flight—for eight minutes during the lift-off. Two Solid Rocket Boosters (SRBs) are clipped on each side of the External Tank; as the name suggests, the fuel they use is solid—a mixture of aluminium and iron oxide powders, stuck together with a polymer. The picture shows how the SRBs and the Shuttle's main engines must all be fired together to lift the whole vehicle's total weight of 1,995,840 kg off the pad. Total thrust needed to do that is 30M Newtons or 3M kg. (A 'Newton' is a unit of thrust named after Isaac Newton, the famous mathematician. 9.8 Newtons of thrust will just balance 1 kg of weight; 10 Newtons will lift it.)

When the vehicle has reached a height of 50 km the SRBs are automatically jettisoned. Small jet motors—four in the nose and four in the tail, push the SRBs safely away from the Shuttle, and parachutes lower them gently into the sea about 280 km from the launchpad so that ships can recover them for re-use.

Usually the Shuttle crew will have other jobs to do as well, for they can carry up to 30 t in their Payload Bay—as many as five smaller satellites, for placing in different positions. If they collect old satellites, or other objects, they can bring up to 14.5 t back to Earth. But when their mission is completed, the crew turns the ship so that the OMS engines are facing forwards, and fires them to act as brakes. That slows the Shuttle down so that it falls back into the atmosphere.

Now it is vital that the Shuttle's computer-controlled instruments, watched by the crew, keep the space-plane in exactly the right position. For as it re-enters Earth's atmosphere the air friction heats up parts of the outside—especially the wings and tail—to 2300°F. The outside is insulated with special felt and silicon tiles or bricks (there are 34,000 of them, and the astronauts' favourite joke is to call the Shuttle a 'flying brickyard'). This keeps the inside cool and comfortable. But if the Shuttle should get into the wrong position at this stage it would get too hot and burn up—and the crew of course would die.

Finally the Shuttle becomes an ordinary aircraft for the landing—but it is an aircraft without an engine. The pilot-astronaut can steer the craft from side to side, like a glider pilot, but he cannot use his engines like a jet pilot and circle the airport for a second landing attempt. However, the computers have worked out the whole re-entry programme from the moment the OMS engines are fired to bring the Shuttle out of orbit so that it will glide down to a smooth landing—usually at either Cape Canaveral or at Vandenberg, the US Air Force base on the opposite side of America in California. From 1982 some Shuttle flights will be launched from Vandenberg, as well as landing there.

Cutaway illustration of Space Shuttle

Section 4   *Inside the Shuttle*

This section shows how different life will be in the new spaceplane, compared with earlier spacecraft like Apollo. The cutaway view at the top shows what will be going on in Earth orbit when the Shuttle is carrying Spacelab, the space laboratory built by the European Space Agency.

On missions like this, there will be three sorts of astronauts. There will be two pilot–astronauts, who can be seen on the top flight deck checking their instruments. There will be at least one Mission Specialist, who is a fully qualified astronaut, and who will usually do any spacewalks (which the astronauts call EVAs, short for Extra Vehicular Activities) which may be required. You can see him at the far right, making an adjustment to the scientific equipment. He has been asked to go out and do that by the Payload Specialist, who is more a scientist than an astronaut, working at his Spacelab console in the centre. On this flight there are four Payload Specialists. The sort of work they might be doing—for instance, making new types of medicine or growing high-quality crystals for use in silicon chips back on Earth—is described in Sections 5 and 6. A second Payload Specialist is floating through the docking tunnel from Spacelab to the living accommodation underneath the flight deck. Two other crew members are preparing for bed. One of their sleeping bags can be seen

20

Astronauts operating manipulator arm

hanging on the wall in the far corner. The doors of the Shuttle's Payload Bay, which would be hinged open, are not shown in the picture.

The open doors can be seen in the close-up views of the Shuttle's nose and flight deck. From inside, the astronauts are operating the manipulator arm, which can be seen pushing a satellite from inside the payload bay out into space. Note that one of the astronauts is a girl, and one is black. The Space Shuttle has been made so that both men and women can become astronauts; and America's NASA is making great efforts to make sure that all sections of their people, whatever their sex, colour or religion, can have an equal share in the Space Age. Another flight deck picture shows how, during launch and landing, the crew will sit just as if they were in an ordinary jet plane. The Commander will be in the usual left-hand seat, his co-pilot on his right. The Mission Specialists will sit behind; if there is no more room on the flight deck, the Payload Specialists will sit in the living quarters below, which will have room for six passengers.

The big airlock and docking tunnel, which can be seen on the left of the picture showing four crew members having a meal, and also with one of them about to float through into Spacelab, is a very important part of the Shuttle. It can be placed in many different positions (as can be seen in the various pictures) according to what sort of mission is being flown.

21

Crew in launch and landing positions

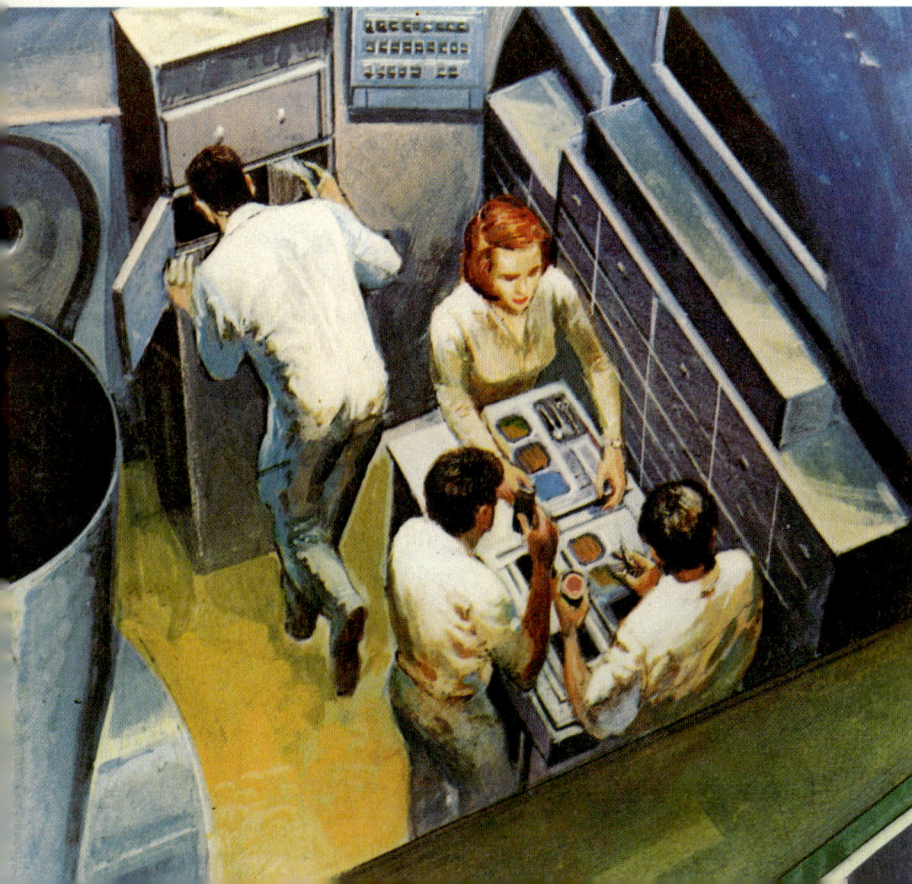

(left) Crew eating

The food they eat

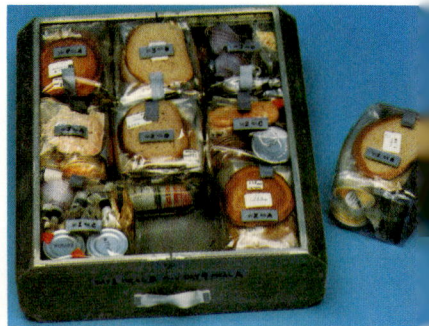

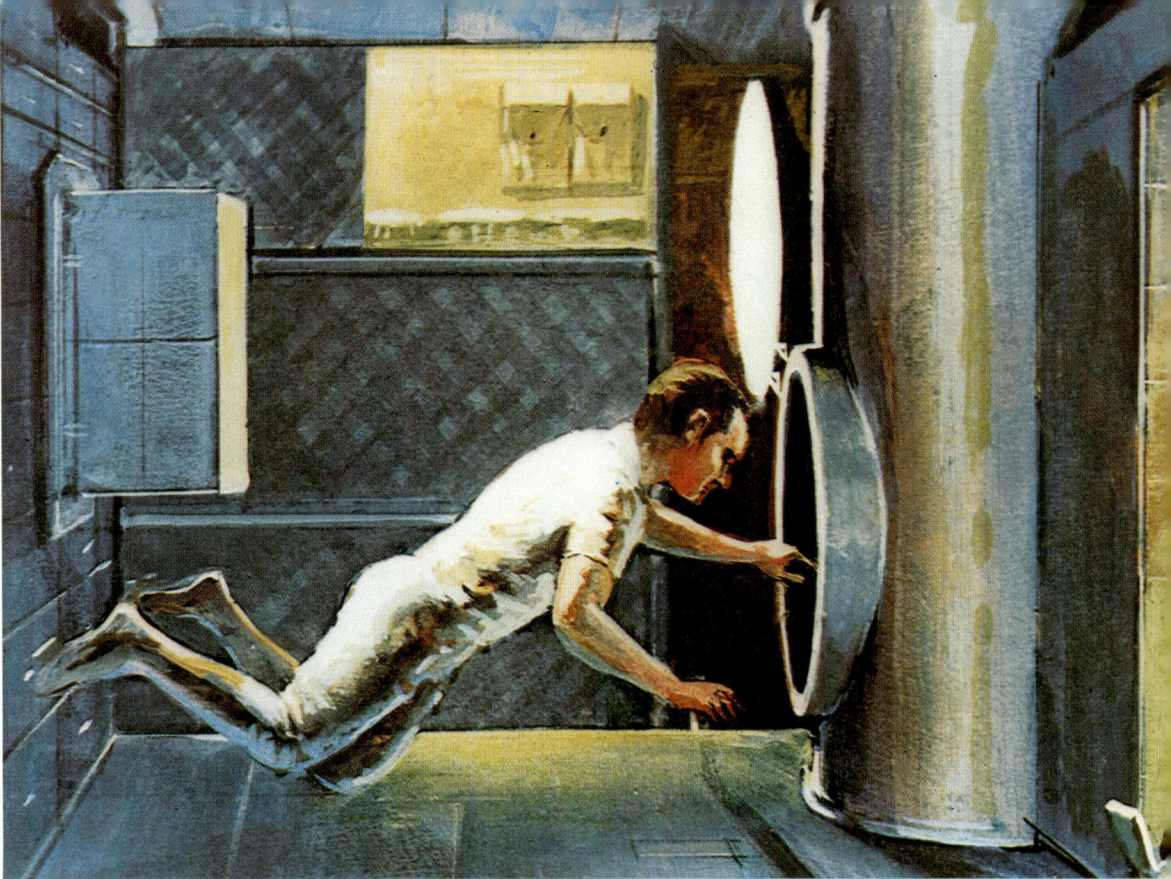

Floating into Spacelab

With the addition of a Docking Module, the airlock can be used for docking the Shuttle to another vehicle—perhaps to another Shuttle, or to a space station, or possibly to one of Russia's Salyut Space Stations if another joint Soviet–American spaceflight takes place. Scientists from the two 'Super Space Powers' have regular meetings to see if it is possible for them to work out joint missions.

Section 5   Shuttle Astronauts

The basic idea of the Space Shuttle is to make it easy for ordinary people to go into space. That is very important, because from now on almost every American satellite will be man-launched. Until now, the 900 US satellites concerned with astronomy, communications, space 'spying', studying Earth resources, and so on, have all been launched by unmanned rockets; only 31 flights have carried men.

The Shuttle crew—Commander and Pilot—will still have to be highly trained astronauts, able, if things go wrong and communications with

Astronauts John Young
and Robert Crippen, Prime
Crew for Shuttle's first
orbital flight

Mission Control break down, to work out with their on-board computers the correct trajectory to fly safely back to base. The Mission Specialists will be scientist–astronauts, and their main task will be operating the remote-controlled manipulator arms and other equipment which will deliver and collect satellites and scientific experiments carried in the Shuttle's Payload Bay.

But unlike the early flights in Mercury, Gemini and Apollo, when launch and re-entry was so violent that the crews sometimes had to endure 9G (that is, their bodies became nine times their normal weight because acceleration and braking was so rapid), Shuttle passengers should never have to put up with more than 3G. This means that the Payload Specialists can be ordinary scientists, doctors, engineers and technicians in reasonably good health. At first they will be given several months' training before the flight; but once the Shuttle is operational it is expected that very little training will be needed at all, apart from instruction in how to cope with Zero-G, or being weightless, and how to avoid becoming space sick. And already plans are being made to carry some journalists, as the first representatives of the public to experience spaceflight.

24

Normally EVAs, or spacewalks, will be done either by the Mission Specialist or Pilot, and two spacesuits will be carried on each flight, selected according to their occupant's size and sex. They are being made in three sizes, small, medium and large, so that they can be easily adjusted for use by different people. This makes them much cheaper than the Apollo suits, each of which was made for a particular individual. Those suits took an hour to put on, and then help was needed from a fellow-astronaut.

The Shuttle suits, made of lightweight fabric, with easily moving joints and gloves so light that it is claimed the wearer can pick up a penny, can be put on in five minutes. A micro-processor, or tiny computer, worn on the chest, checks out the suit to make sure it is safe; and if anything goes wrong it gives a warning signal indicating what the astronauts must do. Although outside temperatures in space vary from $+250°F$ to $-250°F$, according to which side is facing the Sun and which is shielded from it, the astronaut is kept comfortable inside the suit with temperatures which do not vary by more than $2°$.

A more elaborate spacesuit includes the MMU, or Manned Mobility

Preparing for an EVA. After hanging the top half of his spacesuit inside the airlock, the astronaut pulls on the lower half. Crouching down, he gets into the top half like pulling on a sweater. Then, as in a submarine, air is pumped out of the airlock so that he can open the outer hatch and float outside

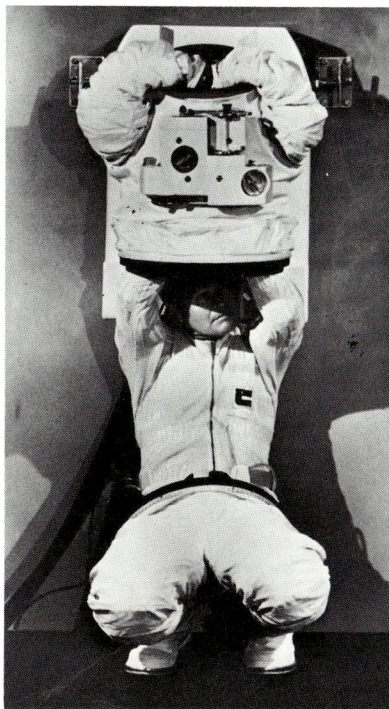

Using handrails to pull themselves along the Payload Bay, crewmen can then maintain the experimental equipment

Unit, first tried out inside Skylab. With this, astronauts are provided with small gas jets so that they can move themselves about in space without being tethered to the Shuttle. MMUs will be increasingly used for carrying out repairs to unmanned spacecraft already in orbit, which need new batteries or refuelling. Later on space-riggers will need them to assemble large space stations and space factories.

And if a Space Shuttle becomes stranded in orbit, it will now be possible to rescue the crew by sending up another Shuttle. Because only two EVA suits are carried, the other passengers will have to crouch in turn inside an 86cm diameter ball. It may not be very comfortable, but it will have its own short-term air supply and radio communications. The ball can be carried across by the space-suited astronauts, or passed along a line connecting the two Shuttles—as in a ship-to-ship rescue, or plucked from the disabled Shuttle's cargo bay by the rescue Shuttle's remotely controlled manipulator arm.

26

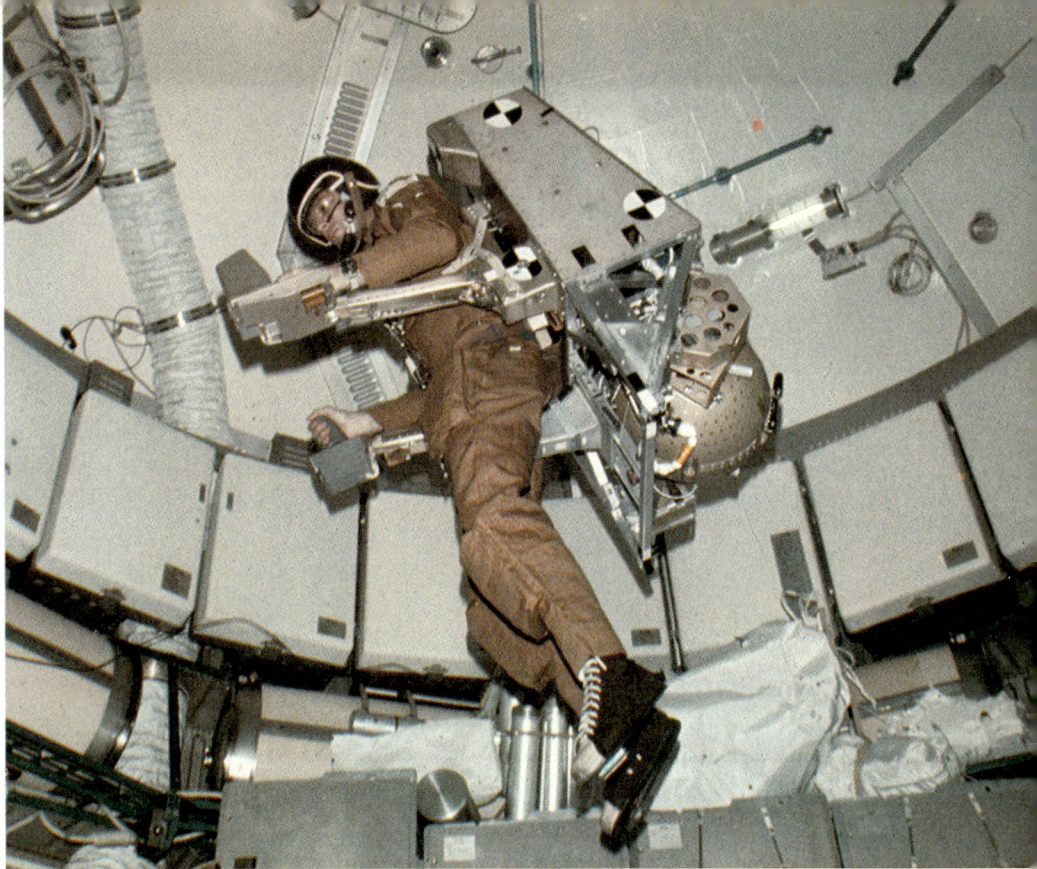

(right) Astronaut Lousma tested the MMU inside Skylab's roomy interior. Its first use is likely to be for repairing any damaged tiles on the Space Shuttle

(below) In a practice rescue, a Payload Specialist climbs into the Rescue Ball, supervised by a spacesuited astronaut

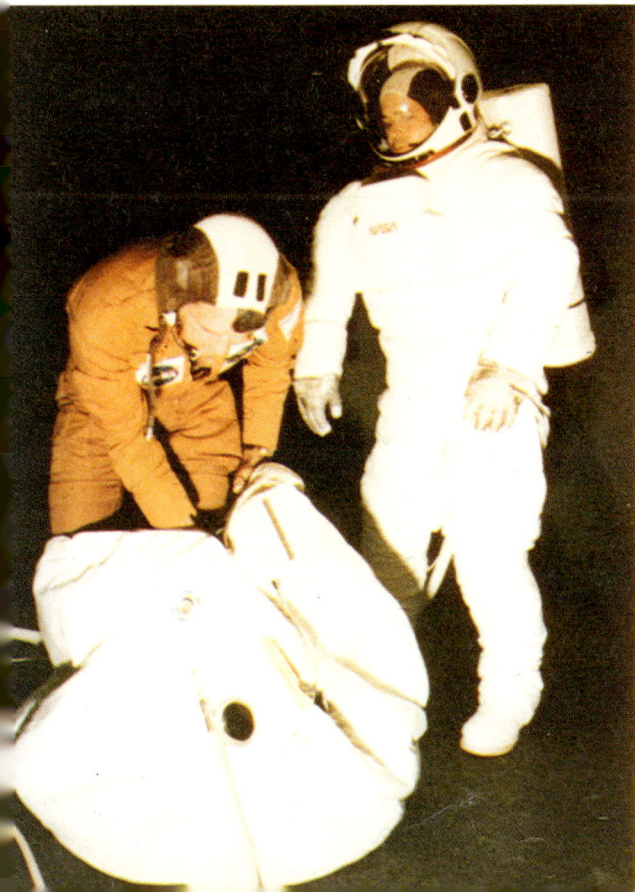

Section 6 Spacelab: Europe's Contribution

Only very large countries, like America and Russia, can afford big space programmes. So in 1973 11 European countries decided to pool the limited amount of money they could spare for space programmes, and set up the European Space Agency (ESA). Its job is somewhat similar to America's National Aeronautics and Space Administration (NASA). ESA, with its headquarters in Paris, builds its own satellites, and usually pays America to launch them, although ESA is now making its own launcher–rocket, Ariane, so that the Agency can launch its own unmanned satellites starting in 1980.

But ESA's most exciting project is Spacelab, the space laboratory mentioned earlier, which is being made as Europe's contribution to America's Space Shuttle system. It can be prepared on the ground for many different space missions, some of them needing four Payload Specialists, and others not needing any men at all. Then, shortly before a Space Shuttle flight, it is just slotted inside the Payload Bay, the docking tunnel and electrical systems are linked up, and it is ready to go.

Spacelab will be carried on over 100 of about 500 operational Space

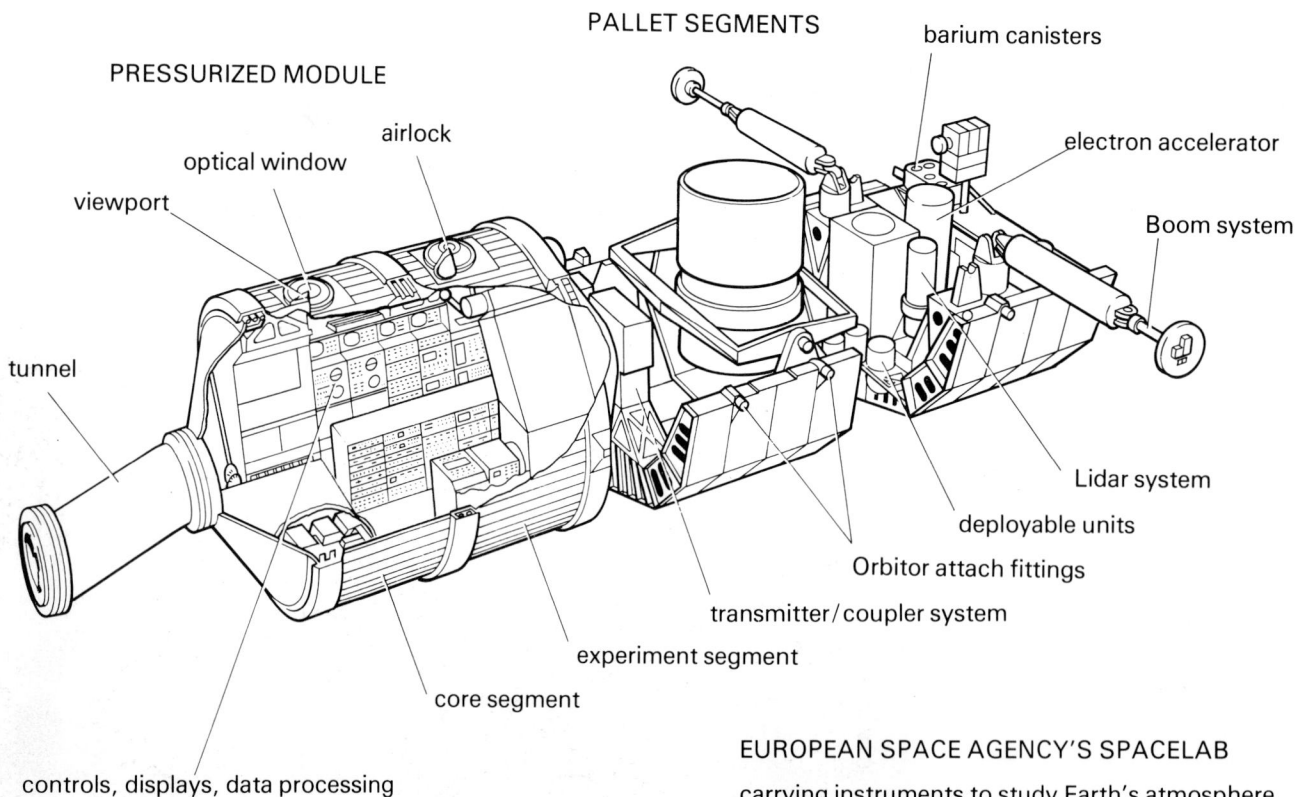

PALLET SEGMENTS

barium canisters

PRESSURIZED MODULE

airlock

optical window

electron accelerator

viewport

Boom system

tunnel

Lidar system

deployable units

Orbitor attach fittings

transmitter/coupler system

experiment segment

core segment

controls, displays, data processing

EUROPEAN SPACE AGENCY'S SPACELAB

carrying instruments to study Earth's atmosphere and Space Physics

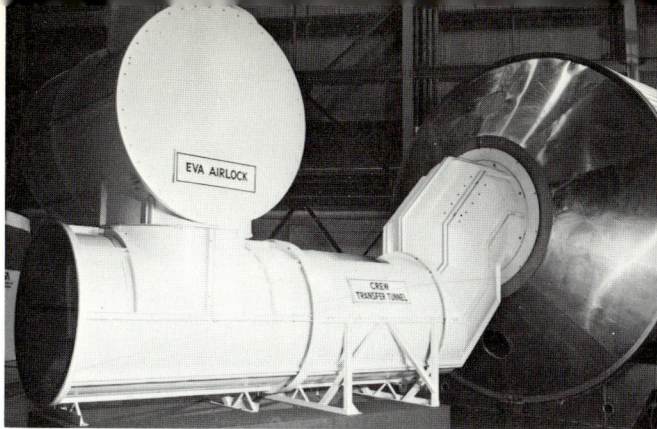

Close-up of Transfer Tunnel linking Shuttle crew quarters to Spacelab's manned section. On top, the EVA airlock is big enough for astronauts to don and remove spacesuits between spacewalks. On each mission two six-hour spacewalks will be possible, plus emergency EVA operations if necessary

Shuttle flights planned between 1981 and 1992. In it men will learn how to operate space factories, using the advantages of Zero-G to make much stronger alloys, and much cheaper and better medicines for things like heart disease, than can be made on Earth. It will also be used to study the Sun and stars, as well as the Earth and its atmosphere, as it is doing in the picture opposite. Plans are being made to use Spacelab 'modules' as sections of permanent space stations.

Spacelab is costing about $700M. Ten ESA countries are sharing the cost. West Germany is paying most: 53.3%; then comes Italy with 18%; France 10%; Britain 6.3%; Belgium 4.2%; Spain 2.8%; Netherlands 2.1%; Denmark 1.5%; Switzerland 1%; and Austria 0.8%.

The first Spacelab flight is planned for 1981; and on board will be the first West European to go into space. He will complete a crew of six; the other five will all be Americans—Commander and Pilot, two Mission Specialists, and one US Payload Specialist. The European will be chosen from a shortlist of three now training for the flight: Ulf Merbold, aged 39, a West German research scientist; Claude Nicollier, aged 36, a Swiss astronomer and pilot; and Wubbo Ockels, aged 34, a Netherlands physicist. (Ages are given for 1980.)

(left to right)   Claude Nicollier, Franco Malerba, Ulf Merbold and Wubbo Ockels. One of these finalists, chosen from 53 candidates from 12 European countries, will become Europe's first astronaut. Malerba, an Italian, has already been eliminated

The Space Telescope is probably the world's most ambitious astronomy project. With it man will be able to look into the far reaches of the Universe. The Solar Arrays are being developed at Bristol by British Aerospace

Section 7   The Space Telescope etc

This section describes some of the exciting Space Shuttle missions already being prepared. One will be the launch of the Space Telescope, planned for 1983. This will enable the astronomers to look seven times deeper into space than is possible with the most powerful telescope on Earth. Perched 520 km above the Earth, well clear of both clouds and our polluted atmosphere, it will at last permit the astronomers uninterrupted views, perhaps as far as the edges of the Universe which includes billions of stars, many of which are believed to have planetary systems similar to our own. One of its jobs will be to help search for life on other planets, as described in Chapter 9. TV pictures from the 2.4m, 9t telescope will be sent to Earth with 2000 scanning lines per picture, compared with Britain's 625-line system, so that the space views will be crystal clear.

It will take the Shuttle crew several days of delicate work with the

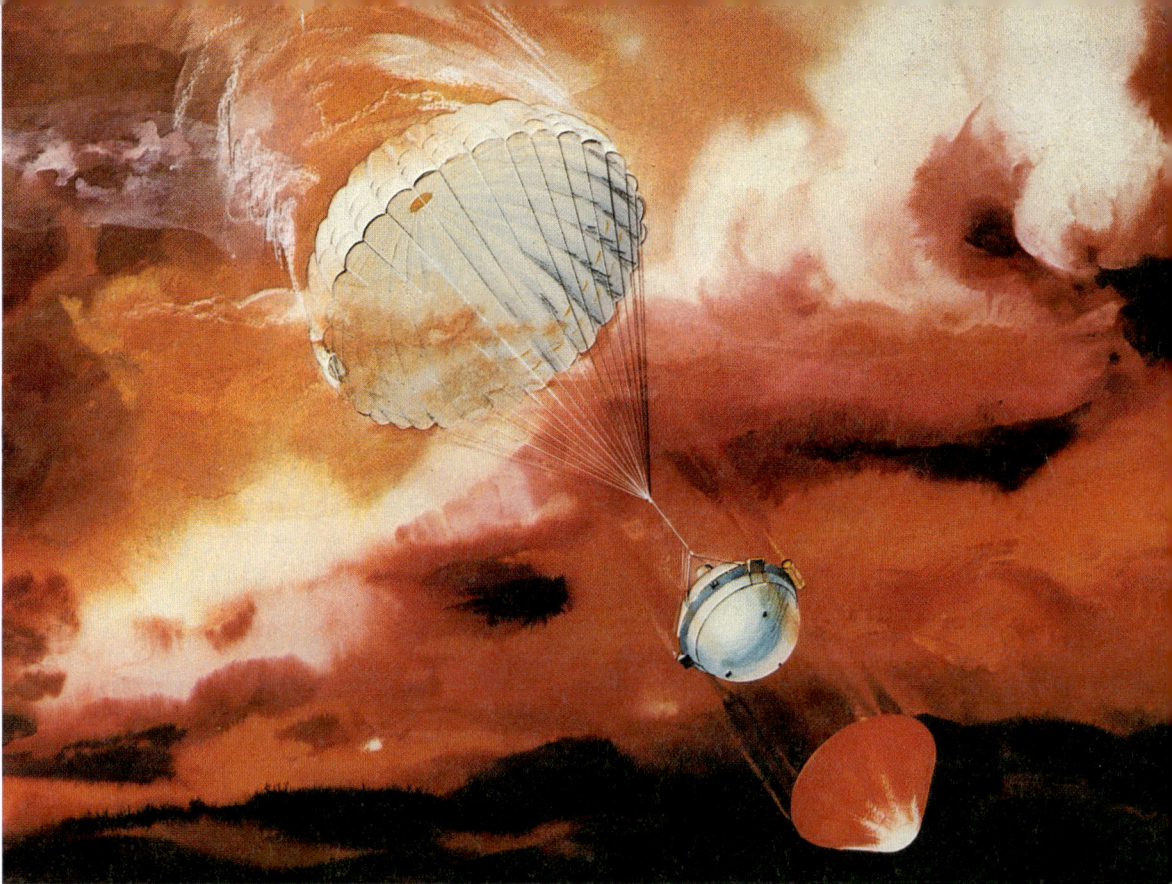

How spacecraft Galileo will sample Jupiter's turbulent atmosphere in 1984

remote-control manipulator arms to erect the Telescope, with its sensitive mirrors and other instruments. Every year or so it will be revisited for maintenance and cleaning, and every four to seven years, brought back to Earth to have its mirrors resurfaced. The European Space Agency is contributing a Faint Object Camera and the huge Solar Arrays. They will cost £13M ($24M) out of the total of £70M ($131M), and that will give Europe's astronomers the right to use it for 15% of the time. But there is so much to look at in the Universe that they, like the rest of the world's astronomers, will have to give one year's notice of what it is that they want to study.

Another important experiment involves a small **Cloud Chamber.** On Spacelab-3, due for launch in mid 1982, it is hoped to find out at last how and why clouds behave as they do: why it is that with two different clouds, which seem to form in exactly the same way, one will bring gentle, nourishing rain, while the other leaves the ground below dry and parched.

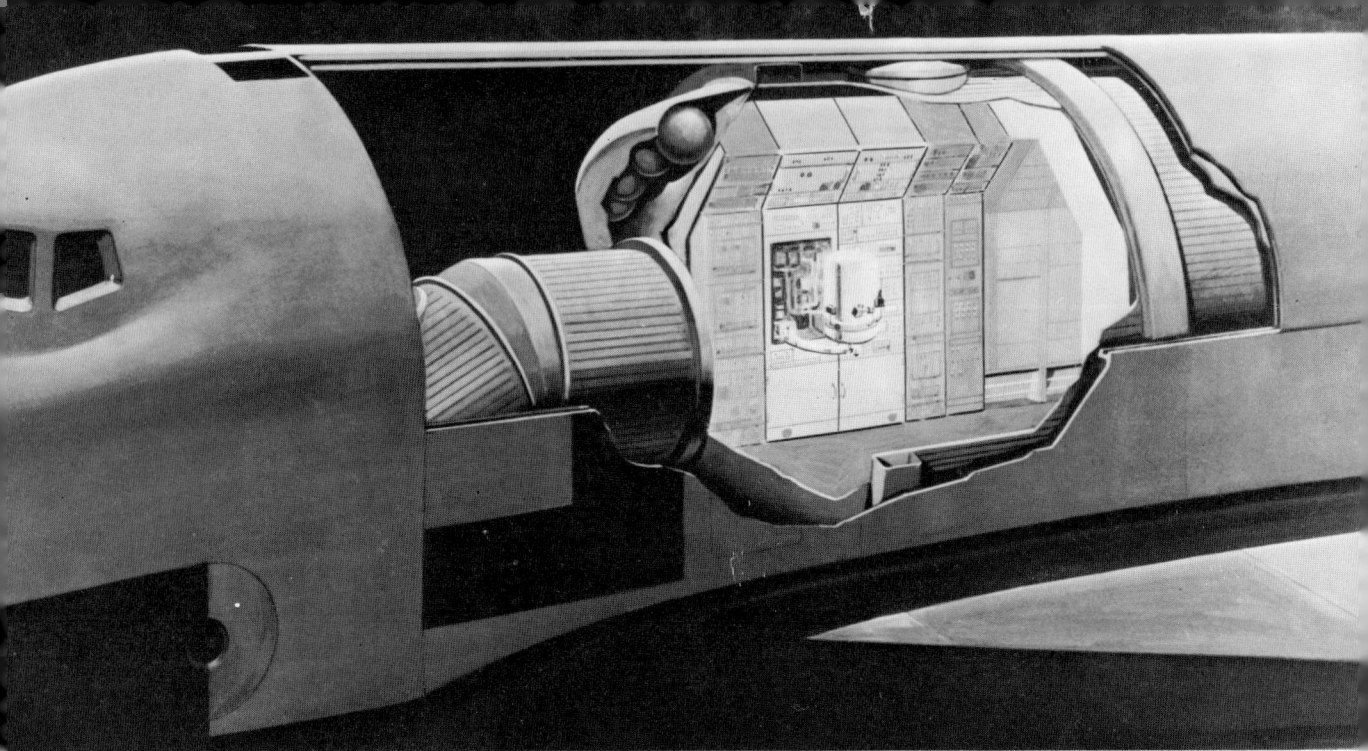

For 35 years scientists on Earth have been trying to capture raindrops, placing them on wax paper, and suspending them on a spider's web. But in 1G conditions they fall to the bottom of the experiment chamber before they can be analysed. They are unable to reproduce the near-weightless conditions in which clouds actually form; at least a million minute particles cluster together to form a single raindrop. What is it that starts these particles—molecules, atoms and elementary aerosol particles—clustering together to form the beginning of condensation?

As the pictures show, the Spacelab Cloud Chamber will be quite small. But in weightless conditions it is expected that the Payload Specialists will be able to produce the exact conditions in which clouds form, and work out the 'microphysical processes' which decide whether or not energy will be released through condensation.

If they succeed it will at last mean really reliable weather forecasts. And the scientists hope they will eventually be able to control clouds—so that instead of deluges which flood crops and houses, the storm clouds can be made to release their water in an area where the water can be controlled and stored as it runs off.

Project Galileo will be the first planetary spacecraft to be launched by the Shuttle. It will be sent off around Christmas 1981, to explore our biggest planet, Jupiter, and some of its 14 moons as well. Named after the 16th Century Italian astronomer who discovered Jupiter's four biggest

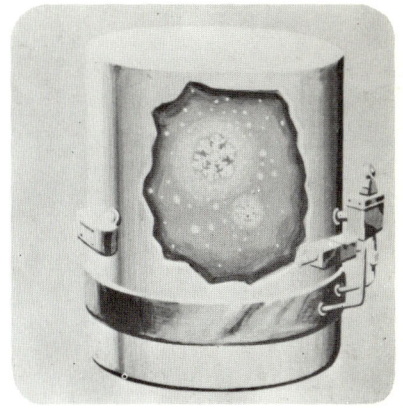

Mission Specialists will use microscopes to watch ice crystals forming in experimental 'Cloud Chambers' to be carried aboard Spacelab (left). They hope to see electric charges developing in their man-made clouds—the processes which affect their growth, size and height, and how much rain they contain

moons, spacecraft Galileo will take 1050 days to make the journey. Part of it will make a parachute descent into Jupiter's multi-coloured cloud layers to send back the first measurements and details before it is destroyed by atmospheric pressures 100,000 times greater than Earth's, and temperatures hotter than those on the Sun. The rest of spacecraft Galileo will go into orbit around Jupiter, and it is hoped that in 1984 it will send us thousands of exciting pictures as well as much other information about Jupiter and its colourful moons.

Section 8   Space Tugs and Power Modules

Like any aircraft or motor car, what the Shuttle can do is strictly limited by the power of its engines, the amount of fuel it can carry, and the weight of its passengers and cargo. So the total rocket thrust for lift-off of 30,802,400 Newtons, or 3,141,180 kg, can only send the Shuttle to a maximum height of 1110 km, and then not with its full load of 30 t. That can only be taken to 185 km, just above Earth's atmosphere. To reach a height of 500 km, the Shuttle can at present carry only 11 t. Plans are already being made to add extra take-off rockets so that the Shuttle can take bigger loads to greater heights—these will often be needed for military satellites. But once the Shuttle has delivered cargoes even to the

Though TRS, shown here as it would have been used to push Skylab into a higher orbit, had to be abandoned, the technique will be used in future Space Tugs

lowest orbital height of 185 km, there are many other ways of moving them around.

About half of the satellites the Shuttle takes into space will have to continue their journeys alone. Most will have an upper stage rocket already attached to them when pushed out of the Shuttle's Payload Bay (see Section 3). After the Shuttle has moved to a safe distance, the rocket will be fired, perhaps to take the satellite on to one of the planets, like the Galileo mission to Jupiter in 1982; or, more often, to a so-called 'stationary' orbit 35,680 km above the equator, to send back weather pictures every 13 minutes giving warning of hurricanes and storms. But there are hundreds of other satellites in lower orbits which need to be captured and inspected, repaired, refuelled, moved, or even brought back to Earth.

The first Space Tug made for this job was called the **Teleoperator Retrieval System** (TRS), a sort of robot sheepdog which the astronauts would control by TV and radio from their consoles at the rear of the Shuttle's flight deck. Although now abandoned, TRS is worth describing because it illustrates what can be done in future. It was designed to be sent across from the Shuttle's Payload Bay to dock with the 90t Skylab space station. That was abandoned in 1973 at an altitude of 400 km after being occupied by three Apollo crews. The idea was that TRS, using an Apollo docking system and manoeuvring engines from the Viking/Mars

34

spacecraft, should push Skylab into a higher orbit to stop it falling back to Earth, so that it could be re-used as a space station when the Shuttle became fully operational. TRS could be controlled by TV for distances up to 0.8 km, and by radio for distances of over 600 km. Unfortunately, because of delays in the Shuttle flight tests, it became clear that Skylab would fall back to Earth before the Shuttle could reach it with TRS. A crew was already being trained for what would have been a most exciting 'space spectacular'. As TRS was quite large and heavy—about 3.2 sq m, weighing 4300 kg when full of fuel—it would have been parked in orbit after use. When needed again, it could be summoned by a later crew of Shuttle astronauts, refuelled and sent off on fresh missions. A more advanced version of this sort of Space Tug is now being designed.

The **Power Module** (PM) is another 'free flying' unmanned Shuttle support system which can be parked in orbit for re-use many times. A

Power Extension Module to gather solar power and enable the Shuttle to stay much longer in orbit

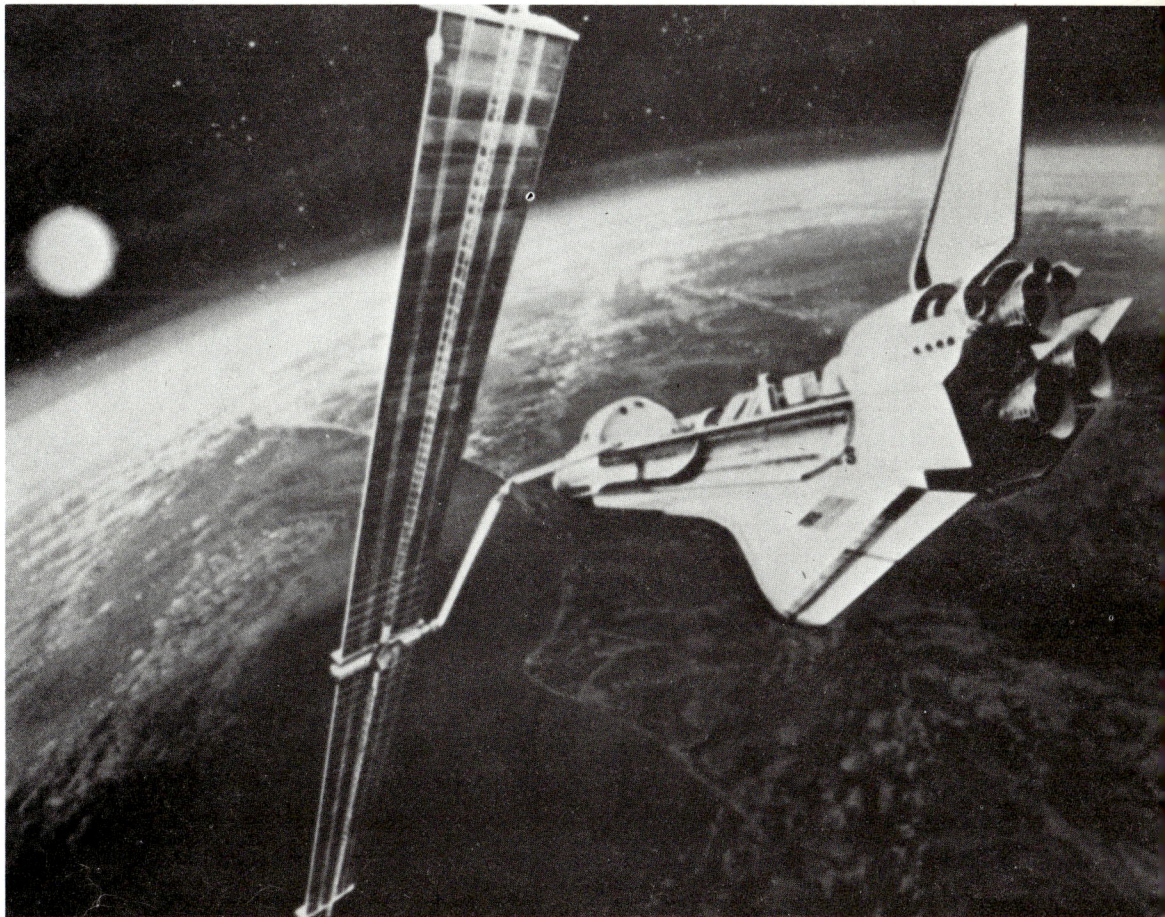

small, orbiting power station due to be operational in 1984, it will collect heat from the Sun through its solar panels and convert it into electricity. A special Shuttle mission will be needed to place it in orbit. Then later Shuttles on long-duration missions will be able to dock with it, and draw from it a steady supply of electricity to power its instruments, and control its movements and air conditioning. Instead of being limited to 30 days, the Shuttle will be able to stay in orbit for 60 days. Ultimately PMs will be used as 'plug in' power stations for many different sorts of space platforms.

The accordion-like solar wing, 32 m long, to be used on the Power Extension Module shown on page 35. When retracted it will fit easily inside the Shuttle's Payload Bay

Another type of Space Tug. After being placed in orbit by the Shuttle, it will be used to send unmanned spacecraft to orbits higher than the Shuttle itself can go

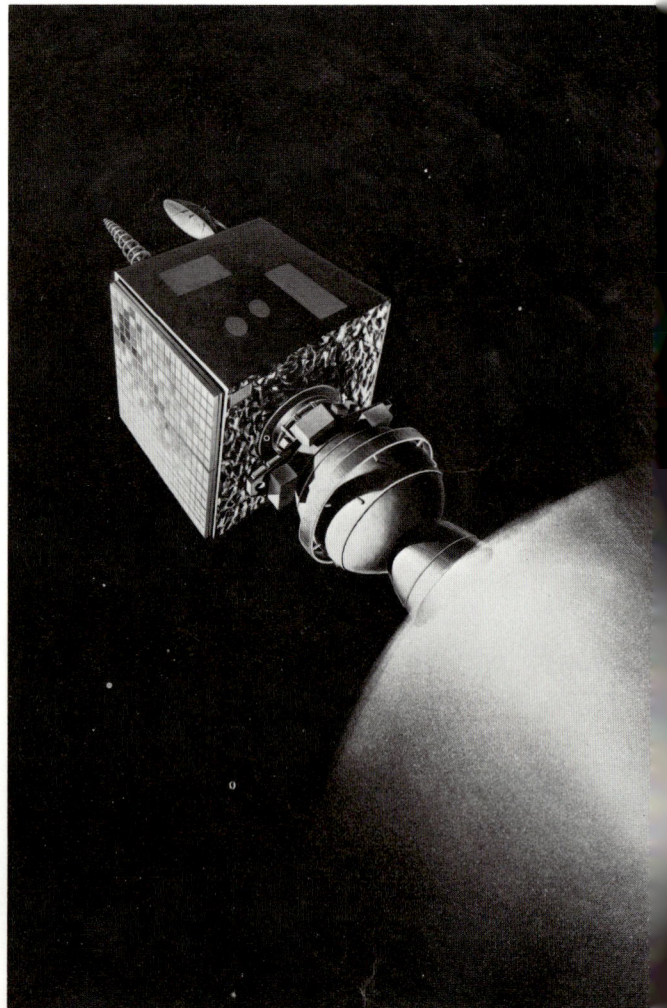

CHAPTER THREE

THE FUTURE IN SPACE

Section 9   Colonizing Space

The previous chapter dealt with missions already planned for the early 1980s. This chapter deals with plans now being made, but not yet given the go-ahead, to enable people in the next 50–100 years, to go out and colonize space. The pioneer astronauts, the intrepid first 100, have done their job: they have made it all possible. All that is needed now is the will (and the readiness to spend manpower and money) to make full use of the opportunities the pioneer-astronauts have opened up. Colonizing space means a new beginning: creating our own brand-new worlds in an ideal environment for our oxygen-breathing bodies. The dreams of the early science–fiction writers like Jules Verne and H G Wells that man would colonize Venus, Mars and the moons of other planets within our own Solar System, may yet come true; it is not impossible that we could restore Mars' lost atmosphere, and reduce the excessively thick, poisonous atmosphere surrounding Venus, so that we could live happily on both. These dramatic changes would be brought about by the controlled use of nuclear explosions—a constructive and useful role, at last, for the atom and hydrogen bombs originally developed as the ultimate weapon for use in Earth wars. But there is a lot of uncertainty about that—we are not sure whether it could be done, and even if it could, whether it would be worth while. Man-made planets may well be more practical and comfortable, and even have a much longer future, than Earth, Mars and Venus.

The fact is that we have the ability and the technology *now* to construct large manned space platforms as a first step. And from them we could progress to creating colonies housing thousands of people, in what is known as Lagrange points. These are areas on each side of the Moon's orbit where the gravitational pull of the Earth, Moon, and Sun cancel each other out—a sort of space 'hole' in which large space stations or colonies could be placed so that they would never drift away, and would

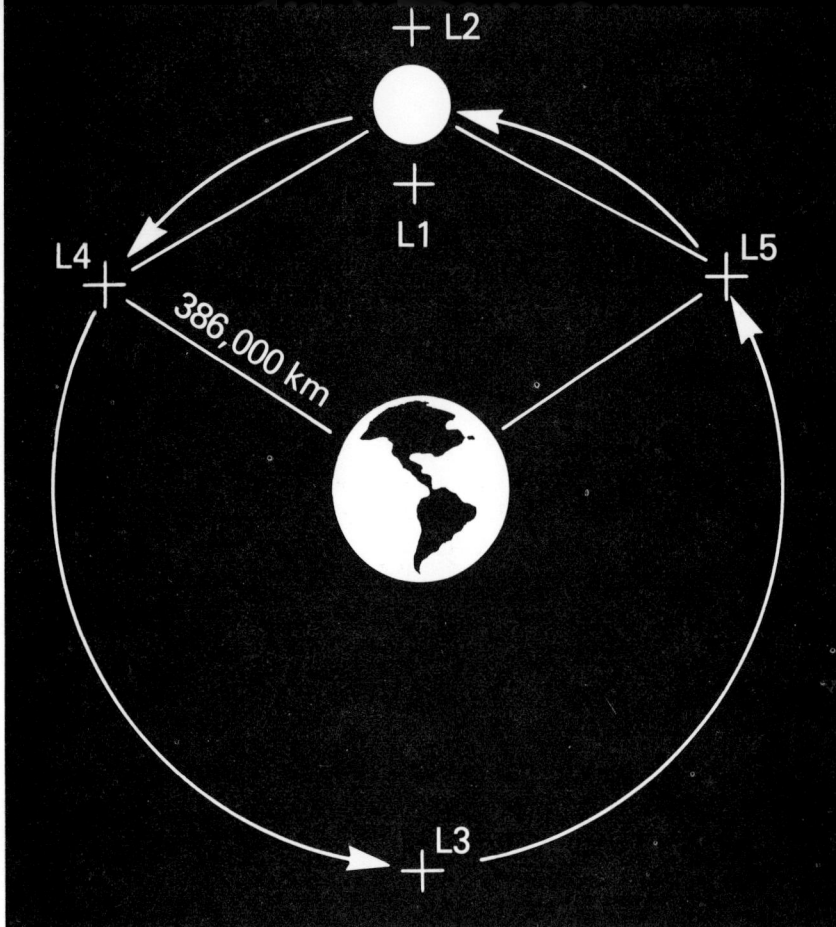

When a small body is orbiting a larger one, as in the case of Earth and its Moon, there are always five 'neutral' points in space at which their gravitational pulls cancel each other out. In the case of the Sun and Jupiter, the Trojan asteroids were found to be trapped in Jupiter's Lagrangian points

need the minimum of thrust to maintain their course and attitude. Other possible sites would be about half-way between Earth and Moon.

From those would come man-made planets which would move outwards throughout our Solar System, making use of the free materials and fuels to be found in abundance in the asteroid belt and on the Jovian and Saturn moons.

And by the 23rd Century, according to science writers like Adrian Berry, man will be moving out to conquer the Galaxy of which our Solar System is part. Mathematicians say the trillions of stars in it should have at least 5 million, and more likely 500 million Earth-like planets with atmospheres of oxygen, nitrogen and water like our own, all ready for human habitation. Maybe some of them will have developed people similar to ourselves already, who may or may not welcome us. (That will probably depend upon how we behave when we arrive!) But in any case there should be plenty of Earth-like planets available for the colonizers arriving in their self-contained man-made planets. By the 2200s, when man will be ready for such adventures, ways may even have been found

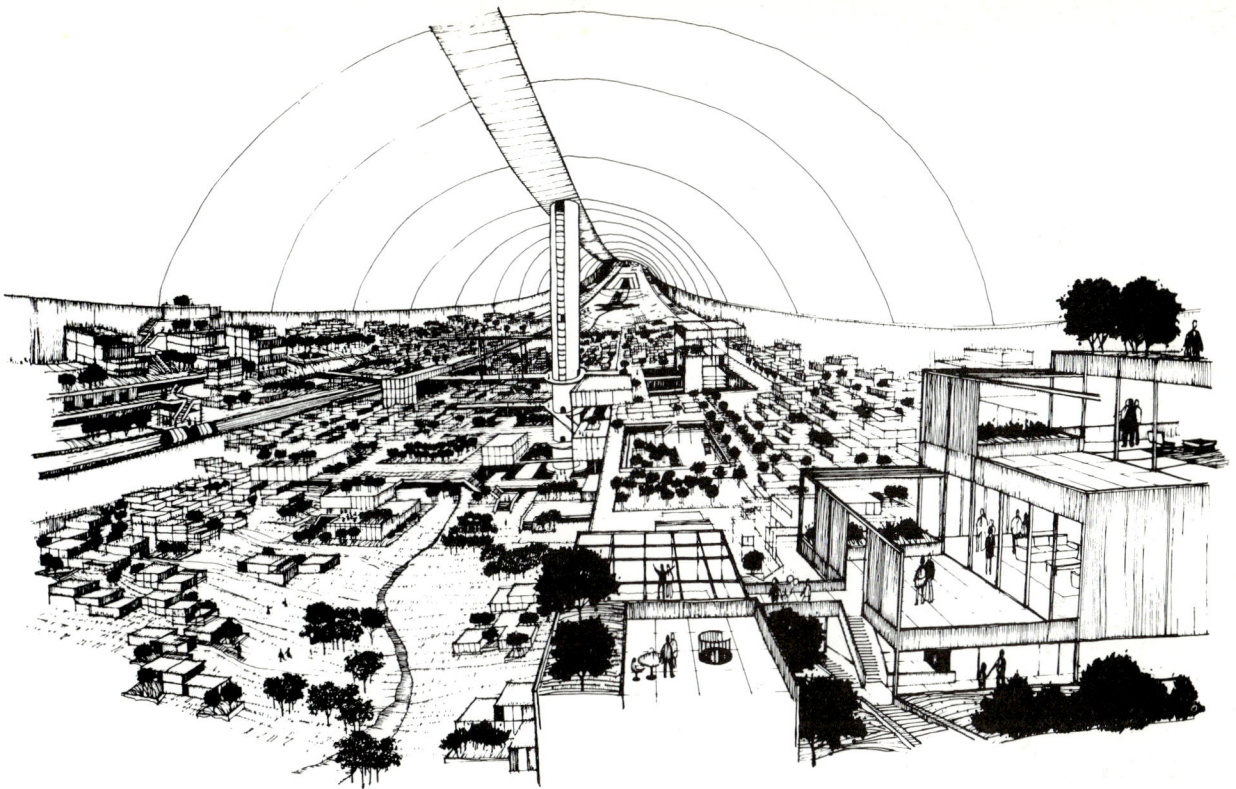

Life in a Space Colony   This NASA drawing shows how houses would be 'stacked' for people living and working in a colony for 10,000 inhabitants. Atmosphere, gravity and sunlight would all be similar to Earth's. Note the elevator shaft in the centre and the flowing river

of reaching other Solar Systems without the need to travel for many years at the speed of light—which is just over 1000M kph.

Section 10   Building Space Stations

Building huge space stations and platforms in Earth orbit is not nearly so difficult as it might appear. NASA already *knows* how to do it. They not only have their own design teams working on the details, but have given contracts to the big American aerospace companies to help to plan them as well, so that when the go-ahead is given by the US Government, they can be quickly built.

A machine able to manufacture the metal beams, or girders, which will be needed to make the framework for big space platforms, already exists. It has been made by Grumman, the American company which built the Lunar Module in which the Apollo astronauts landed on the Moon.

Because everything is weightless, only very light beams will be needed

Beam Builder demonstration on Earth

(left)   Beam Builder operating in orbit

to hold the structures together as equipment is delivered by the Space Shuttle for assembly. Since it would be difficult to manufacture such fragile beams on Earth (they weigh only 1% of comparable Earth structures!), and it would waste both time and space by sending them into orbit in the Shuttle's Payload Bay, it has been decided to manufacture the beams themselves in orbit. And the Grumman machine, called a Beam Builder, will be able to produce *25 km* of triangular beams from just one Shuttle load of rolled aluminium!

As the pictures show, the Beam Builder will produce those triangular beams rather like squeezing toothpaste from a tube. Test beams 12 m long have already been produced during ground tests. In orbit, spools of aluminium only 4 mm thick will be converted by the Beam Builder—which is a robot rolling mill—into beams of whatever length is required; each side of the triangle is 1 m across, and at every $1\frac{1}{2}$ m diagonal and cross braces are clamped and welded into place to strengthen it. A beam 305 m long can be produced from three aluminium rolls, which can be easily reloaded for continuous operation.

In the first orbital demonstration, planned for 1980/81, the Beam Builder will be carried at the back of the Payload Bay, and squeeze its beams into space through the open doors. Later, as the picture shows, the Builder will be left in orbit. It can be used for most of the big space structures now being planned, from large permanently manned stations to huge solar power arrays many kilometres across. As the beams are

40

produced, and cut to the required lengths, astronaut space-riggers operating mobile manipulators—a special type of self-contained mobile spacecraft—will manoeuvre them into position and join them up. These manipulators are being designed by Boeings, at present better known for their Jumbo Jets.

Section 11   Solar Power Stations

Some of the many different proposals for Satellite Power Stations are illustrated here. With America already beginning to run short of power, many scientists think these projects should be given top priority. But it is fair to add that other equally prominent space scientists have doubts about their practicability. Rockwell's design would be more than 30 sq km in area. After being assembled in low Earth orbit, it would be moved very slowly (to avoid stressing the huge structure) over a period of six months into stationary orbit. Solar cells would convert the Sun's heat into electricity, which would be beamed to Earth by microwave transmission. Huge receivers, which would be above the ground, sea or lakes, would convert the microwave energy back to pollution-free electricity. But 180 of these huge satellites would be needed just to supply one quarter of

Constructing a solar power station

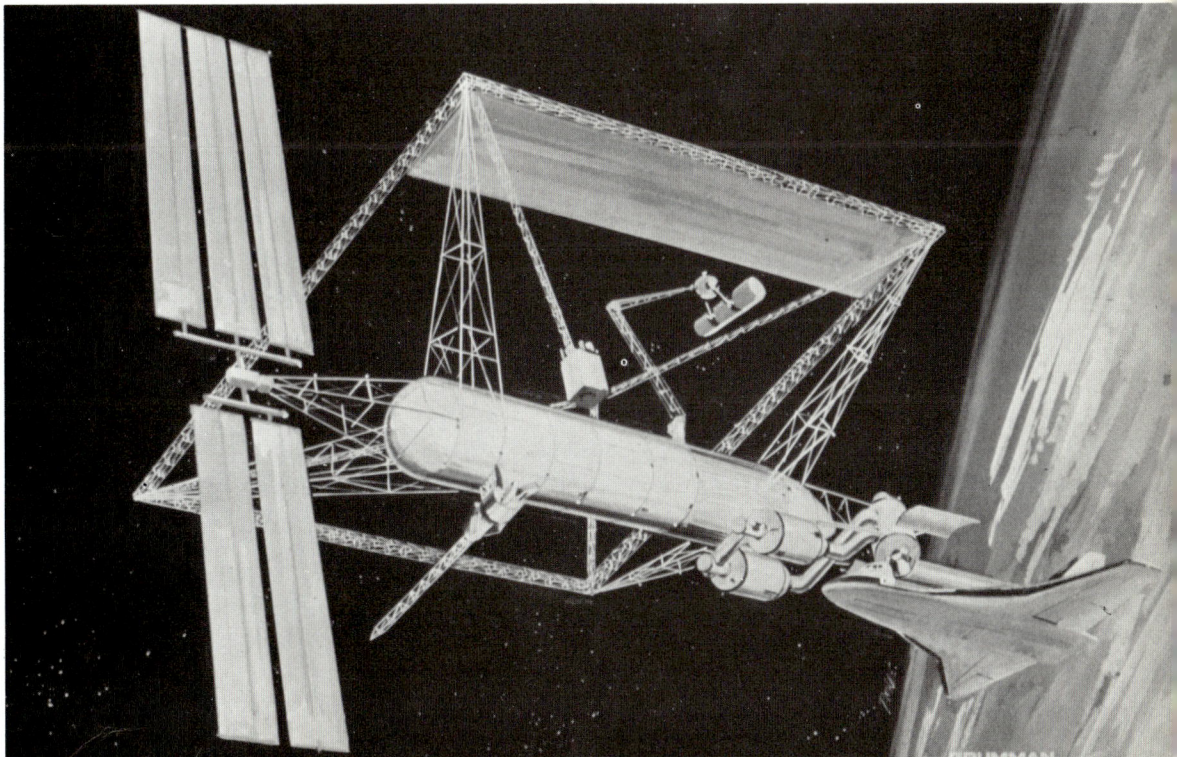

SPACE SOLAR
POWER CONCEPT

GEOSYNCHRONOUS ORBIT

Solar power station at work

America's electrical requirements. We are assured that the microwave
transmission would be of such low power, and spread over such a large
area, that no harm would come to aircraft or birds flying through them;
and cattle, it is said, could safely graze beneath the ground-based receivers.

Section 12   Why We Need Space Factories

Why bother with space factories? The answer is that many things can be
produced better and more economically in space than on Earth. Factories
in orbit, therefore, won't compete with those on Earth, but produce things
that Earth factories can't. Thus, in addition to supplying the needs of their
own space colonies, they will be able, like any healthy community or
country, to export their products back to Earth. Zero gravity, which is
impossible to simulate on Earth, and a complete vacuum (which is very
difficult and expensive to create on Earth in pressurized chambers) mean
that products can be made in conditions of cleanliness and purity
unthinkable on Earth. And because there is no atmosphere, space factory

Shuttle operating typical Space Processing Facility

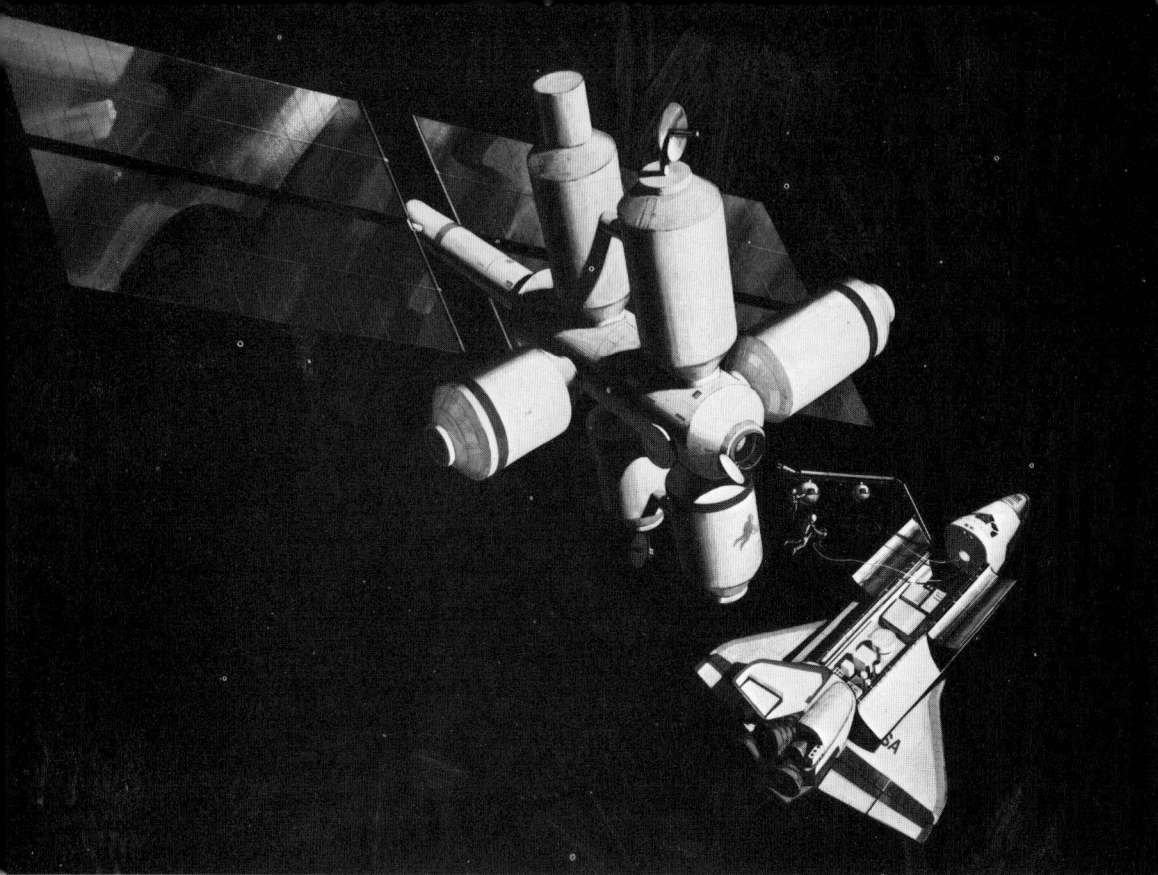

Shuttle docking with Space Factory

machinery will operate indefinitely without corrosion or wear. The Russians did the first experiments in space welding in Soyuz 6 in 1969, and 10 years later were operating quite advanced, if still small, furnaces in Salyut 6. American scientists expect private companies to be operating fully developed commercial facilities, which will make a profit, by the early 1990s.

Both Russia and America have already worked out techniques for making new alloys—mixtures of metals and other materials—in pilot space furnaces. By melting samples of different metals and injecting gases into the mixture, extraordinary new materials can be produced: for instance, steel as light as balsa wood. Glass and steel, impossible to mix on Earth, can be combined in orbital factories. And glass itself can be produced in unique qualities. Much improved lenses will mean far better telescopes, microscopes and cameras—and better spectacles too.

The Earth-produced crystals which are increasingly needed for miniaturized processing systems always contain some flaws. 1G conditions, for instance, cause them to pick up contamination from the container

44

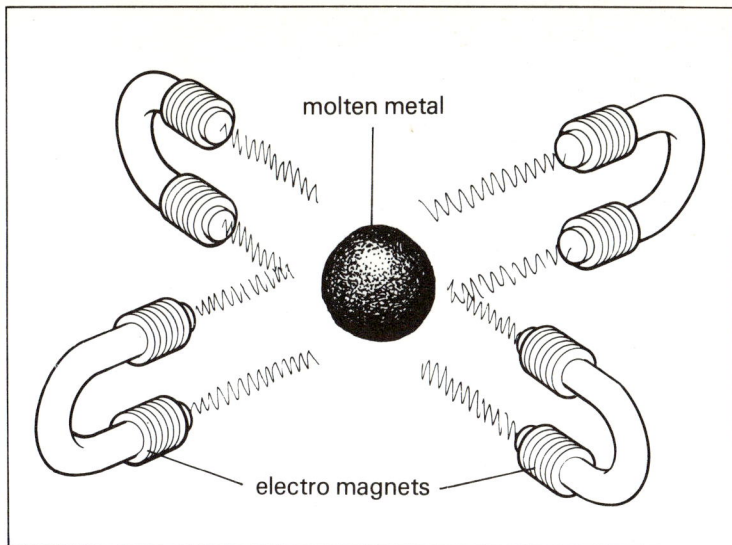

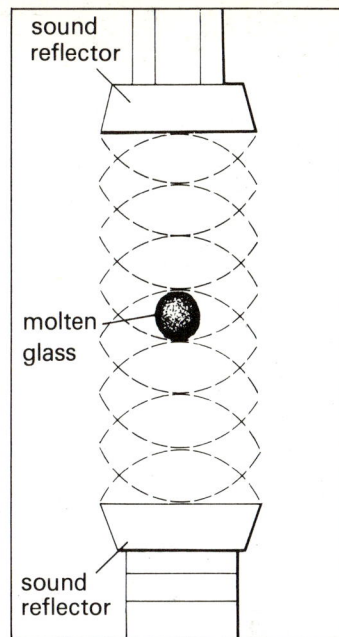

How materials can be heated and mixed in space without using a container

(left)   Magnets keep the molten metal in position

*(right) Non-magnetic materials like glass held in place with sound waves.
Scientists call it 'an acoustic vice'*

walls; and of course the molten material always tends to pick up the shape of the container which holds it. In space, where everything 'floats', what is called levitation processing will ensure that materials are evenly distributed and mixed. Large, near-perfect crystals can be formed. Heating and handling the materials suspended in space will obviously need special techniques. Electromagnetic coils surrounding the materials will heat them uniformly, whereas, of course, when they rest in a pot with the heat beneath, the pot diverts the heat around itself. Metals can be held in position with magnets; non-magnetic materials like glass can be held in position acoustically, with sound waves.

Processing facilities like this are expected to be of great benefit not only to the computer and electronics industry, but to lead to further advances in medicine and communications. Around them a new industry turning out products worth $2 billion a year is expected to develop within about a decade. German scientists think that 80% of the materials we will be using in the year 2000 have not yet been invented—but *will* be invented in space factories.

Section 13   *Quarrying Materials from the Moon*

As yet, few people really believe that large structures like space colonies inhabited by thousands of people, or even solar power stations, are really possible. It involves, of course, assembling millions of tonnes of materials in Earth orbit. But strangely enough, this is not nearly as big a problem as it may appear. And the solution was originally proposed by the famous science writer Arthur C Clarke more than 25 years ago.

Most of the material won't come from Earth at all. It will be quarried from the Moon, and launched into orbit from there by the 'mass driver' system described below. All the same, especially in the early stages of construction, there will be a need to launch much larger weights from Earth than even the new Space Shuttles can deliver when making continuous flights. NASA, together with the aerospace firms like Rockwell and Boeing who work for them, are already designing more advanced versions of the Shuttle—unmanned Cargo Spaceships, also called Heavy Lift Launchers. The simplest version would enable the Shuttle Orbiter to deliver 60–90 t compared with 30 t now. By using four instead of two SRBs, loads of over 100 t could be orbited; and there are even long-term plans for getting loads of up to 500 t into orbit by using what the scientists call 'Big Dumb Boosters'.

But when it comes to space colonies, even loads like this will only supply the sophisticated equipment, like space furnaces, computers, environmental systems and nuclear power stations which in the early stages will have to be made on Earth to get the colonies started. No one is proposing to send

Boeing Artist's conception of a two-stage Heavy Lift Vehicle taking 270,000 kg of cargo from Cape Canaveral into low Earth orbit. Cargo is in top stage. Both stages would fly back for re-use

off millions of tonnes of earth and fertilizers to get the all-essential space farms started (though it *will* be necessary to start these spaceborne Noah's Arks with breeding cattle from Earth).

At this point many people may ask: but why not colonize the Moon itself, which is already there and an inexhaustible source of raw materials? Well, though an essential source of materials, the Moon itself has many disadvantages. First, because of the need to lower far more equipment and people on to the lunar surface, and then use Moon-based rockets to get the people and their products back into lunar orbit for return to Earth, transport would cost twice as much as for space colonies. Then, although it does provide near-perfect vacuum conditions for space manufacturing, the one-sixth lunar gravity is a major problem. The advantages of weightlessness, freely provided in space, are not available on the Moon; and for human beings, one-sixth gravity is not enough to keep muscles and bone in good condition without taking a great deal of exercise. Against that, it is relatively easy to obtain normal gravity—1G—in the main habitation areas of the space colony by rotating it. And finally life on the Moon would not be very pleasant, since there are two weeks of continuous sunshine followed by two weeks of darkness. That two-week day–night cycle would also make crop growing difficult.

Nevertheless, manned lunar bases will be an essential part of the whole operation. Perhaps 100 Moon miners will be needed to operate it—a rugged life for fit, strong men spending much of their time in spacesuits. They will rotate between the comforts of the space colony and periods of perhaps 6–12 months on the Moon—probably in the southern part of the Sea of Tranquillity. It will be the sort of life that oilmen lead now in Alaska.

Space colonies have been made possible by the six Apollo Moonlandings and careful analysis of the 385 kg of lunar soil brought back by the astronauts. We know that the soil contains abundant quantities of aluminium, magnesium, titanium, iron, glass and oxygen. The job of the Moon miners will be to keep this raw material flowing out to the growing space colonies at the rate of a million tonnes a year.

This will be done by what Professor Gerard O'Neill, the American space scientist, has named a 'mass driver'. Simply explained, it is a circular conveyor-belt which can accelerate small bucket loads, each containing about 18 kg of soil and Moonrock, along a sort of railway track, and hurl them into space at lunar escape velocity of 2.4 kilometers per second (8640 kph). The bucket itself will slow down and be brought back on its

track to pick up another load and send that off perhaps two minutes later. A steady stream of such buckets will keep the material flowing—like a stream of meteorites. As in any rocket launch, their course will be precisely computed and guided, so that they will be 'caught' by a large cone-shaped collector. That is likely to be stationed at L2, the Lagrangian point about 80,000 km behind the Moon's farside. When full, the collector, or skip, would be replaced with another and towed by a robot space tug to the colony at L5—a journey taking perhaps two months.

What is going to drive the buckets, enabling them to sling their loads into space in this miraculous way? This is the development referred to at the beginning of this section. Arthur Clarke's solution was based on the idea of a Frenchman 60 years ago—'dynamic magnetic levitation' he called it. The buckets would be propelled by magnetic impulses driven by electric energy through a conducting guideway. The secret is that the magnetic fields result in less drag as the buckets go faster, instead of more which would be the normal effect. And on the Moon's surface a great advantage is that only 1/22 as much energy is needed to reach escape velocity as is needed on Earth. Professor O'Neill has already built and successfully tested a small version of the mass-driver. Electricity will be needed to drive it. A nuclear power station will have to be sent to the Moon to get it started; and later, solar power stations, turning the Sun's heat into electricity, will be built—preferably two of them, so that when one is in darkness the other will be in sunlight.

(left) This painting by Pierre Mion shows the railtrack which would be used to launch bucket-loads of moonrock into orbit. Material would be scooped up by vehicles, probably remotely controlled, such as the one in the foreground

(right) With support from NASA and help from his students, Professor Gerard O'Neill (seen here in centre) built this working model of a mass driver, which by using pulsed magnetic fields, accelerated small buckets from zero to 128 kph in one-tenth of a second

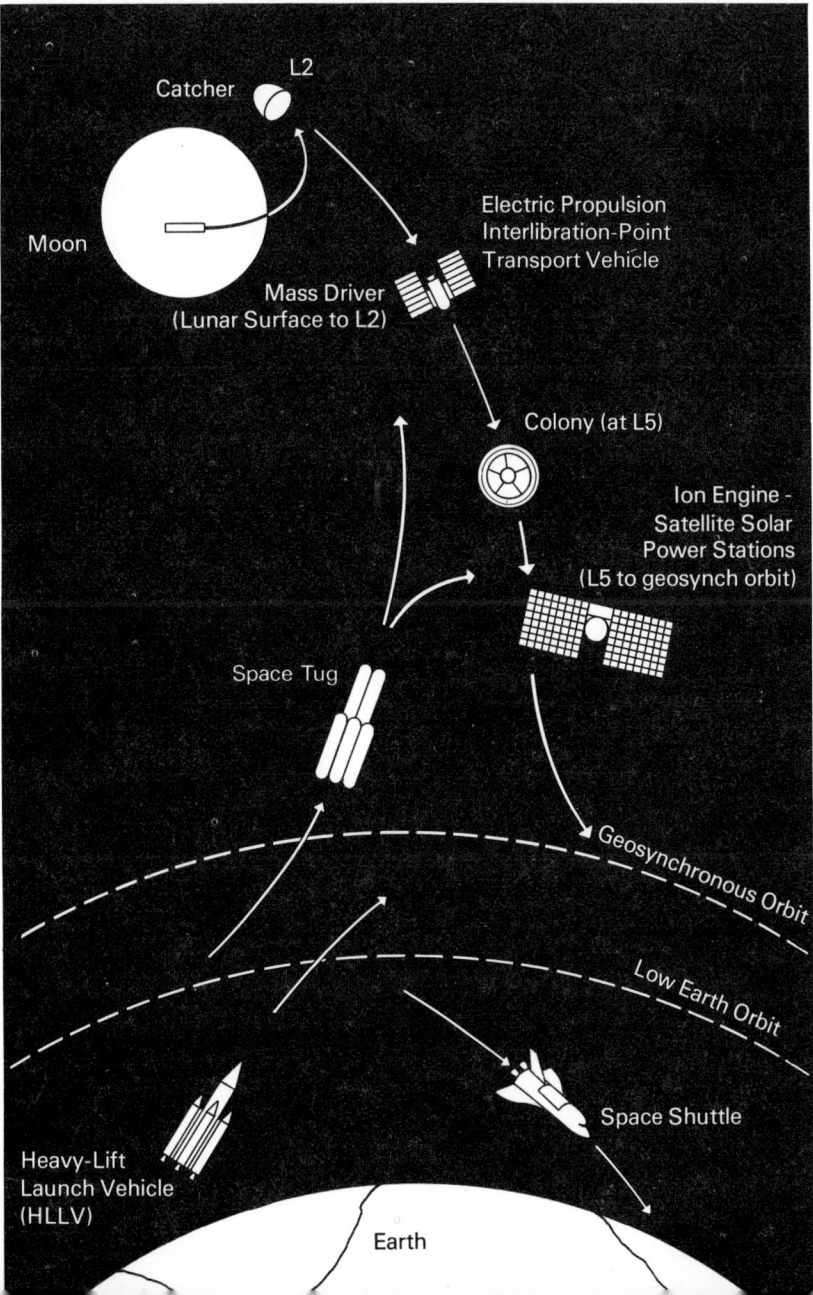

Catcher — L2

Moon

Mass Driver
(Lunar Surface to L2)

Electric Propulsion
Interlibration-Point
Transport Vehicle

Colony (at L5)

Ion Engine -
Satellite Solar
Power Stations
(L5 to geosynch orbit)

Space Tug

Geosynchronous Orbit

Low Earth Orbit

Heavy-Lift
Launch Vehicle
(HLLV)

Space Shuttle

Earth

Building a Space Colony. While building materials are quarried from the Moon, Space Shuttles deliver men and technical equipment to Low Earth Orbit. Space tugs take them to the colony from there

'Wheel-like' space colony for 10,000. About 2 km in diameter, its covering of Moonrock protects the inhabitants from radiation. The mirror floating above reflects sunlight into the interior. Attached at the bottom is the facility for melting lunar ore with solar heat and extracting oxygen, metals, etc

Once it has arrived at the processing factory, none of the precious lunar ore will be wasted. A solar-powered smelting plant will extract the aluminium and silicon for the colony's superstructure and windows, the oxygen for its atmosphere, and so on. Some of the rubble left over will be used on the outside to shield the residents against radiation and meteorite hits, just as the Earth's atmosphere protects us from these things; and the rest can be turned into soil for the colony's farms. In his book *The High Frontier*, Professor O'Neill has described in great detail how the first space colony, which he has called 'Island One', could be built. It would house 10,000 people and take 10 years or more to build once the first space processing factory was established. He thinks that in 200 years' time there could be more people living in space than on Earth.

50

CHAPTER FOUR

MAN IN SPACE: How He Got This Far

Section 14   Cosmonauts versus Astronauts

So far only two countries have sent men into space—Russia and America. By the end of 1979 Russia was expected to send up her 50th cosmonaut; America's 50th astronaut was expected to be launched in 1980. China will probably be the third country to send men into space, because she needs to catch up with the Russians in the military use of what the late President Kennedy called 'This New Ocean'. Because manned spaceflight costs so much, all the other countries are at present content for their first spacemen and spacewomen to 'hitch' rides aboard either Soviet or American spacecraft.

Russia, of course, sent the first woman, Valentina Tereshkova, into orbit as long ago as June 16 1963; but at present has no more women cosmonauts. America, on the other hand, now has six women astronauts among their trainees and the first of these may go into space aboard one of the five Shuttle flights planned for 1980/81. The European Space Agency's six astronauts also include one woman who could be aboard the second Spacelab flight in 1982.

Although Russia and America carried out a very successful joint flight in 1975, when Apollo and Soyuz spacecraft docked in orbit, and Soviet cosmonauts and American astronauts spent three happy days together, they are still racing one another to be first with new space techniques. That is partly for military reasons (as explained in Chapter 8); but even more because Russian scientists as well as Americans think there will be many benefits for mankind as we improve our space technology.

While America beat Russia in the race to land men on the Moon, the Russians have sinced moved well ahead with the development of their space stations. Since America's last Skylab crew in 1973 spent a record 84 days in space, the Russians have beaten that three times: with stays of 96 and 140 days by the Soyuz 26 and 29 crews in 1977, and of 175 days by the Soyuz 32 crew in 1979, all in the Salyut 6 space station.

*Russia's first 11 cosmonauts   (left to right) Vladimir Komarov (killed in Soyuz 1);
Konstantin Feoktistov; Yuri Gagarin (first man in space; later killed in air crash); Alexei
Leonov (first spacewalker); Herman Titov; Valery Bykovsky; Valentina Tereshkova (first
woman in space); Pavel Popovich; Pavel Belyayev (died from illness); Boris Yegorov; and
Andrian Nikolayev (who married Valentina)*

It has been neck-and-neck ever since the Soviet–American space race
started on April 12 1961, when Yuri Gagarin made his historic first one-
orbit flight. America began her spaceflights only a few weeks later; and as
the years passed, sometimes one country was ahead, sometimes the other.
America moved rapidly ahead when disaster overtook Russia's Soyuz 1
spacecraft, which crashed in 1967, killing Cosmonaut Komarov; and
again when the three-man Soyuz 11 crew was killed in 1971. But America
had her own tragedy: the first Apollo crew was burnt to death on the
launchpad, also in 1967.

The six-year gap between the end of America's Skylab space station
missions in 1973 and the start of the Space Shuttle flights gave Russia a
chance which she did not miss. She moved far ahead with an unbroken
series of Soyuz flights to her Salyut space stations; and by the end of 1977
at last overcame the problems she had had for years with docking. Now it
seems likely—but is by no means certain—that the Space Shuttle will put

This painting by Leonov shows Voskhod 2 with its telescopic docking hatch

the Americans ahead once more. But we know that Russia too is developing her own Space Shuttle, as well as much larger space stations.

Section 15 Russia's Manned Flights

Vostok Six flights were made by Russia's first spacecraft, which was a fairly simple sphere, most of its payload, or weight, being used up with all-round heat-shielding, to make sure it did not get burnt up during re-entry. The last of these flights carried the world's first woman into space— Valentina Tereshkova. At the time of writing she is still the only woman to have made a flight. Soon after her flight Valentina married Cosmonaut Nikolayev, who had flown in Vostok 3; and their daughter, Elena, the world's first 'space baby' proved to the scientists that there were no harmful after-effects for those who made spaceflights.

Voskhod In 1964 three cosmonauts were squeezed into an improved Vostok spacecraft; it was such a tight fit they could not carry any spacesuits, and it is believed the flight was made on the orders of Mr Krushchev, then Soviet Prime Minister, so that Russia could claim the 'first' three-man flight before Apollo flew. The second and last Voskhod carried only two men, and was notable because Cosmonaut Leonov made the world's first spacewalk. He was outside Voskhod for just 15 minutes.

Soyuz   Then, starting in 1967, the Russians began using the famous Soyuz spacecraft, and have averaged $2\frac{1}{2}$ flights per year ever since. It was intended to be a three-man space ferry; but the re-entry module is so small that three men could not squeeze into it when wearing their bulky spacesuits. So, although spacesuits were taken up in the Soyuz's orbital module, for spacewalks and other activities in orbit, they had to be left behind for the return to Earth. But the day came when the Soyuz 11 crew were all killed because pressurization failed during their return from a very successful 24-day flight; had they been wearing spacesuits, they would have been perfectly safe. So the Russians had to reduce the crew to two, so that spacesuits could be worn for all important manoeuvres, until it became possible to make Soyuz bigger. There have been many failures during the Soyuz flights; crews repeatedly found themselves unable to dock with the Salyut space stations (see Section 15) and until the end of 1977 Soviet space scientists must have had a very depressing time. On what was meant to be Soyuz 18 the launch rocket went wrong, and the cosmonauts had to make an emergency landing before getting into orbit. They narrowly escaped coming down in China—and of course relations between Russia and China are not at all friendly.

But suddenly, with Soyuz 26, things started to go right for the Russians. Docking troubles were overcome, and history was made with the first double docking. In January 1978, with Soyuz 26 already docked at one end of the Salyut 6 space station, Soyuz 27, with another two-man crew, docked at the other end. That crew came home in the Soyuz 26 spacecraft, so that the first crew, who stayed up for a record 96 days, would be able to use a fresh spacecraft when they did return. That was because, if Soyuz 26 had been left 'powered down' for three months in the bitter cold of space, its systems might not have worked properly when it was needed for the return flight. Now long-stay crews in Salyut space stations can be regularly visited by short-stay crews, who often include a cosmonaut from Czechoslovakia, Poland, or one of the other Soviet-bloc countries. The Russians have also perfected the technique of sending up unmanned Soyuz spacecraft, called 'Progress', filled with fuel for Salyut's manoeuvring engines and with fresh oxygen, food and other supplies. The resident crew unloads the supplies, refills Progress with their rubbish, and casts it off to burn up in the atmosphere as it re-enters. That frees the second docking

54

Salyut space station mockup, at 1979 Paris Air Show. Progress cargo ferry is docked at left; Soyuz spacecraft docked at right. First Sputnik can be seen top right © *Flight*

port for more visitors. Progress can deliver enough supplies for two men for over 40 days.

By the end of 1978 the Soyuz 29 crew had raised the long-duration record to 140 days; and the Soyuz 32 crew had settled down to what was expected to be at least a six-month flight. They came home after 175 days, however, after doing an emergency spacewalk to release an experimental radio-telescope which had become jammed on the cargo docking port. This seemed to end suggestions by Russian scientists that Salyut 6 might be kept manned almost continuously for five years.

Salyut Space Stations   Since Russia launched Salyut 1 in 1971, there have been (at the time of writing) six of these 18·5 t space stations. With one Soyuz spacecraft attached they weigh 25 t; with two the weight is over 30 t, and the total length over 30 m. And though even then the weight is only one-third of America's famous Skylab space station, the Salyuts are much more versatile. But Russian space scientists had many

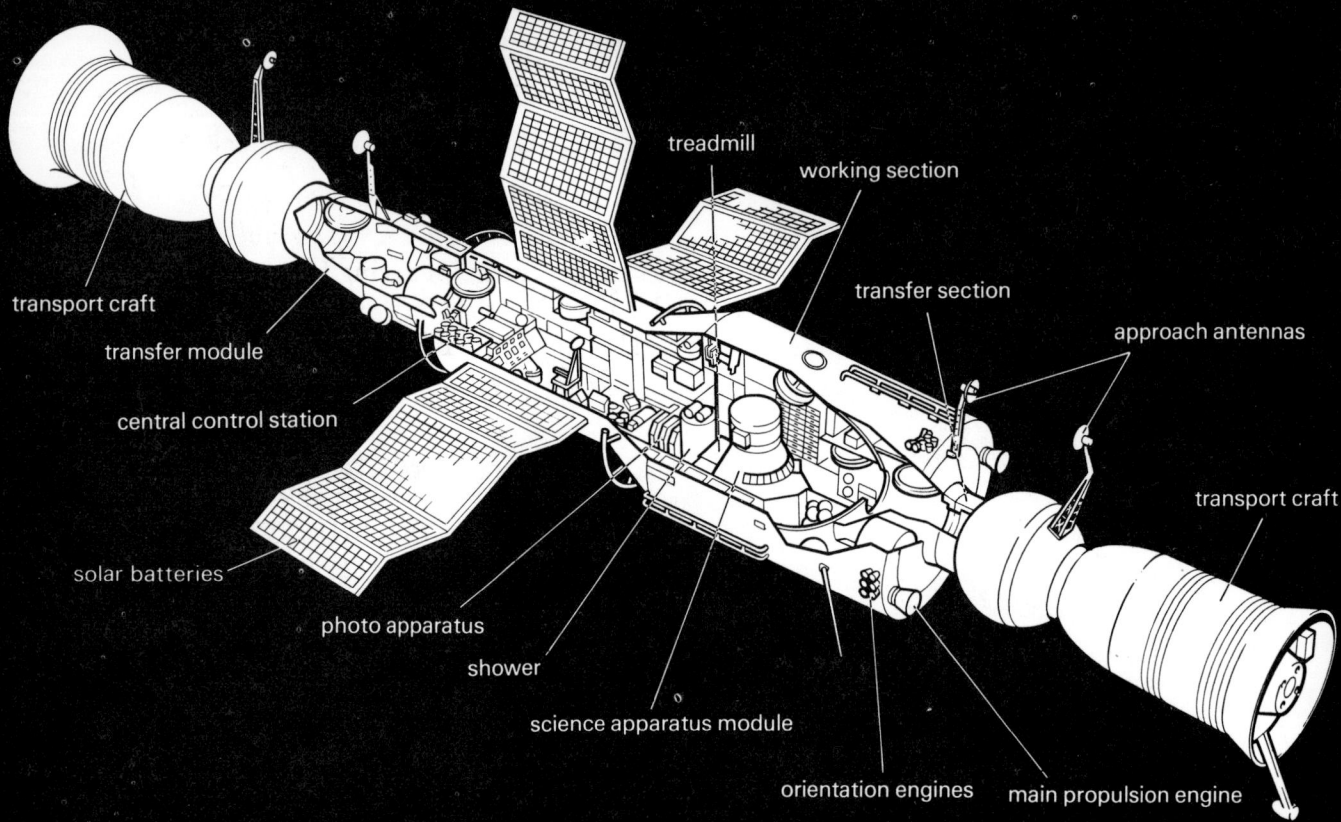

Labels on diagram:
transport craft
transfer module
central control station
solar batteries
photo apparatus
shower
science apparatus module
treadmill
working section
transfer section
approach antennas
transport craft
orientation engines
main propulsion engine

Cutaway drawing of Salyut 6 complex showing compartments

difficulties with the early Salyuts. The second went out of control and broke up before men could go aboard. And until they learned from America during the joint Apollo–Soyuz mission, the Russians were never very successful with docking. Even Salyut 6, launched in September 1977, had a bad start. Soyuz 25, which was supposed to deliver the first crew, collided with Salyut instead of docking, and had to make an emergency return to Earth. But since then 15 spacecraft have been successfully linked with it—seven manned and one unmanned Soyuz, and seven unmanned Progress ferries. And as this book was going to press the two Soyuz 32 cosmonauts had been aboard for over 150 days.

It has three habitable compartments, as the pictures show; and since each Soyuz also has three smaller compartments, by the time two Soyuz craft are docked at each end, the whole 'space sausage' has a total of nine rooms. So, if one of the cosmonauts wants to go off on his own for a while, there is no problem!

The reason why Salyut has such a long life is that, every time it begins to fall back to Earth, it can use its rocket engines to push itself higher, into a safe orbit again—and of course fresh supplies of fuel for those engines are regularly delivered by the Progress ferries. In addition, Progress can also be used as a Space Tug, by using its own engines to push Salyut higher. This has been done several times. It has the advantage of saving Salyut's own rocket fuel, and using up the fuel on board Progress which would otherwise be wasted when it is cast off and burnt up in Earth's atmosphere.

Section 16   Cosmonauts at Work

Although Russia's cosmonauts have not yet reached the Moon, they are now far ahead of America in developing the ability to live and work for long periods in space. About 50 have been trained so far, and on September 23 1978, Cosmonauts Vladimir Kovalenok and Alexander Ivanchenkov became the world's first spacemen to spend 100 days continuously in orbit. When they finally returned to Earth in November, they had set a new long duration record of 140 days. During that time, too, the total number of days spent in orbit by all Russia's cosmonauts had passed the 1000 mark, compared with the American astronauts' total of 937 at the end of the Apollo–Soyuz flight.

What had they been doing during those 1000 days? Broadly speaking, six different things: (1) Learning to live and work in Zero-G without damaging their health. (2) Learning to use weightlessness to make new metals and alloys. (3) Studying Earth's resources with the help of special cameras. (4) Studying the Sun, and how it affects us on Earth. (5) Studying astronomy—the distant worlds outside our own solar system. (6) Studying the military use of space, especially for 'spying', or reconnaissance as it is more politely known.

So far as (1) is concerned, the cosmonauts have been very successful in developing various types of space suits, particularly one they call the Chibis vacuum suit. With closely fitting rubberized trousers, these suits draw the blood into the legs, just as gravity does on Earth, and they start wearing them a few days before returning to Earth. They have also learned that the best way to keep fit in space is by taking exercise for about

Before their 96-day flight in the Salyut 5 space station, Cosmonauts Romanenko and Grechko tested their new EVA suits in a water tank

two hours every day; they do this by using their space 'bicycle' and also by walking on a 'treadmill', or moving belt, to which they fasten themselves with rubber straps over the shoulders. These pull them down with exactly the same force as gravity pulls us down on Earth.

The Soyuz 26 cosmonauts also used a new type of semi-rigid suit, with self-contained breathing equipment in backpacks, for a spacewalk outside Salyut 6 at the end of 1977. That was necessary to see if Soyuz 25 had caused any damage when it collided with the space station in its unsuccessful attempt to dock. Although the Soyuz 29 cosmonauts also did a spacewalk to collect samples of materials placed outside Salyut 6 to see if they were suitable for making future space stations, the cosmonauts were still far behind America in EVA experience at the beginning of 1979. But by the time this book is published it is likely that that too will have changed, since the Russians appear to be pushing ahead faster than America with plans for bigger and more advanced space stations.

There are separate sections in this book about space factories, and other activities mentioned above.

58

Section 17 America's Manned Flights

Mercury Like Russia, America began her manned flights with a tiny one-man capsule. But Mercury was bell-shaped, with only the bottom of the bell heat-shielded. Weight had to be kept to a minimum because at that time only the Redstone rocket (thrust 347,000 Newtons) was available to launch it. Again like Vostok, Mercury was originally designed so that it could be entirely controlled from the ground; but the astronauts were soon proving that there were times when only the on-board pilot could save the mission from failure. In 1961 Alan Shepard and Gus Grissom made brief 15-minute up-and-down test flights before John Glenn became the first American in orbit in 1962 (see *The Observer's Book of Manned Spaceflight* for Log).

Gemini Looking very similar, the two-man Gemini spacecraft was in fact twice the weight and much more advanced. US astronauts had to put up with two flightless years between the last Mercury and first Gemini flight. But then 10 Geminis were flown at the rate of five a year in 1965–6. America put 20 men into space while Russia achieved only the

MERCURY SPACECRAFT
To Larger Scale

WEIGHT
Launch : 1935 kg
Orbit : 1355 kg
Retrofire : 1347 kg
Splashdown : 1311 kg
Recovery : 1099 kg
(MA 6 weights)

Escape
Tower

Antenna
Housing

Recovery
Compartment
(Parachutes)

Crew
Compart-
ment

Heat
Shield

Retrograde
Package

(left)   This tiny Mercury spacecraft (seen attached to the Launch Escape Tower) carried Alan Shepard, America's first spaceman, on his 15-minute up-and-down flight

Ed White, who died later on the Apollo launchpad, making America's first spacewalk on Gemini 4

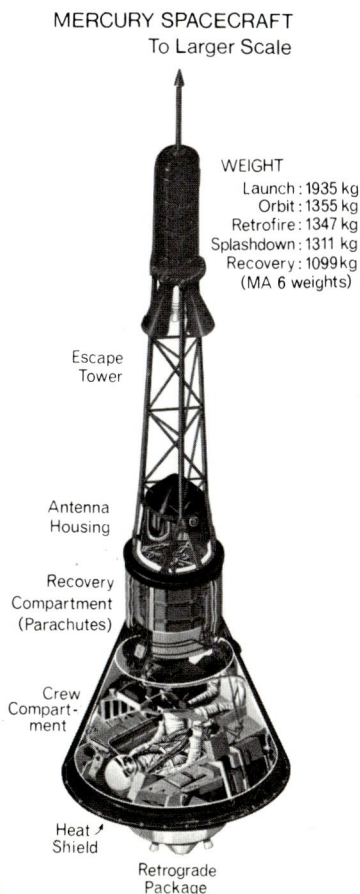

last two-man Voskhod flight. Long-duration flight, rendezvous with other vehicles, docking, spacewalking and guided re-entry were all mastered. On Gemini 8 Neil Armstrong (later to become first man on the Moon) and David Scott did the first space docking—a historic event which enabled Americans to step on to the Moon, and more than a decade before the Russians achieved a docking. The achievement was hardly noticed at the time because Armstrong and Scott had to make an emergency return when their Gemini spacecraft, linked to an Agena target rocket, went out of control.

Apollo   The famous three-man Apollo spacecraft was first suggested by NASA in 1960 for flights around the Earth and Moon. But in May 1961 President John Kennedy set the American nation this challenge: Land a man on the Moon and bring him safely home before the end of the decade. The spiderlike Lunar Module, astonishingly like a Moonlanding vehicle suggested by the British Interplanetary Society many years earlier, was hurriedly designed for Apollo to take to lunar orbit, there to be released to land two men, while the third waited for their return in Apollo. In January 1967, when Gus Grissom, Ed White (who had made America's first spacewalk on Gemini 4) and Roger Chaffee were burned to death in a Cape Canaveral launchpad fire just before they were due to make the first Apollo test flight, it seemed quite impossible for America to reach the Moon in the 1960s. In fact it would never have been achieved *without* that tragic fire. During an 18-month delay, the whole Apollo system was redesigned, and all sorts of faults which had been worrying the astronauts were put right. It was October 1968 before the first manned flight took place. Then Frank Borman, James Lovell and William Anders made history at Christmas that same year by becoming the first men to fly round the Moon. Borman's Christmas Day reading from the first chapter of the Bible, Genesis, with the whole world listening as they circled the Moon, will never be forgotten. And only seven months after that Neil Armstrong, Edwin Aldrin and Michael Collins were launched by the mighty Saturn 5 rocket in their 45t spacecraft on their great adventure—a 102-hour journey to the Moon, and three hours walking on the lunar surface. The unfortunate Mike Collins had to wait in Lunar Orbit while Armstrong and Aldrin undocked and descended. Manoeuvring to find a safe landing place among the boulders on the Sea of Tranquillity, Armstrong finally brought down *Eagle* (as they had named the Lunar Module) with only 2% of the descent fuel left. 'That's one small step for a man, one giant leap for

*(above)   The first space 'rendezvous'. Gemini 6 meets
Gemini 7 in December 1965, 250 km above Earth*

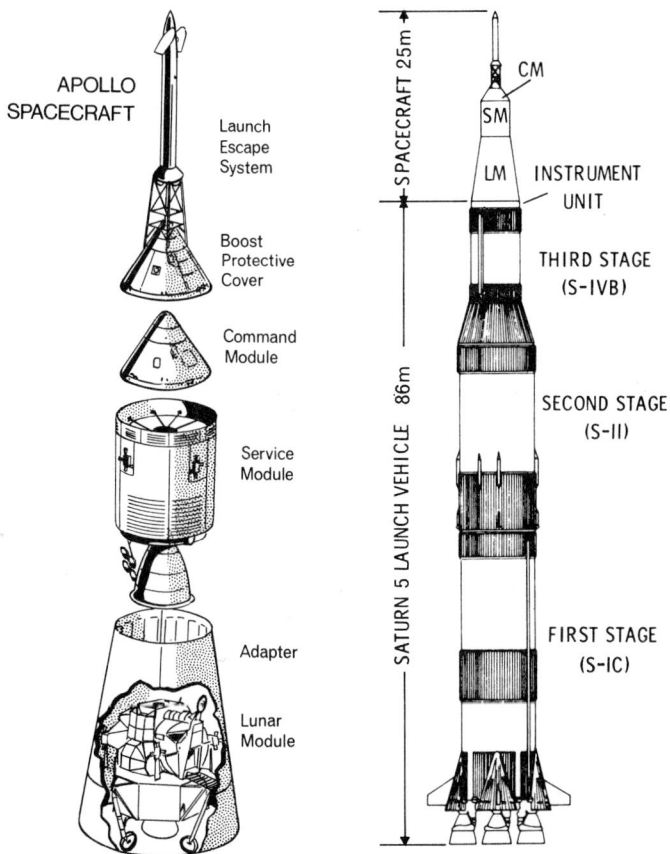

APOLLO
SPACECRAFT

Launch
Escape
System

Boost
Protective
Cover

Command
Module

Service
Module

Adapter

Lunar
Module

SPACECRAFT 25m

CM

SM

LM   INSTRUMENT
       UNIT

THIRD STAGE
(S-IVB)

SECOND STAGE
(S-II)

SATURN 5 LAUNCH VEHICLE   86m

FIRST STAGE
(S-IC)

Neil Armstrong and Edwin Aldrin (seated), the first men to land on the Moon on July 20 1969. Michael Collins (centre) stayed aboard Apollo 11 in lunar orbit until they rejoined him for the 400,000km journey home

mankind,' said Armstrong, as he became immortal by becoming the first man to step on the Moon. They brought back 21.75 kg of rock and soil amid world-wide rejoicing when they splashed safely down in the Pacific Ocean.

Nine more Moonlandings had been planned, so that many different areas of the Moon could be explored. But in the end, only five took place. Apollo 13 was a near disaster, when an explosion 330,000 km from Earth destroyed its oxygen tanks; Jim Lovell, Thomas Mattingly and Fred Haise, hoping to become the third crew to reach the Moon, had to be content with flying round the farside. Using the Lunar Module and its engines as a liferaft, cold and very short of oxygen and water, they were brought safely back to Earth in a massive rescue operation. Apollos 14, 15, 16 and 17 were all very successful; but the last three Moonlandings were cancelled to save money. Project Apollo, which cost $24 billion finally

The last Saturn 5 rocket, taking the Skylab space station into orbit

came to an end in October 1977, when five robot scientific stations, placed on the Moon by the Apollo 12, 14, 15, 16 and 17 crews to send back information about Moonquakes and other events, were shut down. Apart from the ground fire, not one life was lost during this most ambitious and hazardous of all man's journeys of exploration.

Skylab The Skylab Space Station, weighing 90 t, was launched in May 1973, and visited in turn by three Apollo astronaut crews, who set new records by living in it for periods of 28, 59 and 84 days. Severely damaged by excessive vibration when launched unmanned by a Saturn 5 rocket, one of its huge solar wings was torn away, and the other jammed shut; in addition, the shield intended to keep its big workshop cool, as well as protect the men inside from micrometeorite hits, was torn away. At first it seemed that the whole $2400M project, prepared by 26,000 scientists

63

and technicians, would be wasted. But, as in Apollo 13, the ingenuity of ground staff, and the determination of the astronauts, turned disaster into triumph; by the time the third crew splashed down on February 8 1974, America had demonstrated not only that men could live and work in space almost indefinitely, but also that faulty equipment could be replaced, and repairs improvised. Astronaut Pete Conrad, who was the overall Skylab Commander, went up 10 days late with the first crew, docked after much difficulty, and then led a spacewalk. Standing on top of Skylab's workshop with a rope over his shoulder, he pulled open the jammed solar panel, restoring Skylab's power supplies; and he and astronauts Joe Kerwin and Paul Weitz succeeded in pushing a 'parasol' sunshade through the experimental airlock to take the place of Skylab's sunshade until a more permanent shade could be erected by the second crew.

In the end, as one astronaut said: 'Skylab worked better broken than anybody had hoped for if it was perfect'. The three crews brought back information and data on which scientists will work for years: their Earth observations included 40,000 pictures and 80 km of magnetic tape readings; studies of the Sun included 182,000 frames of film showing unique details of solar flares and coronal holes. On-board experiments with melting, welding and brazing of metals, and with the production of

Skylab as it was finally abandoned in orbit. Note the improvised 'sunshade' and the fact that one solar wing is missing

new metal alloys and crystals, provided invaluable preparation for setting up Space Factories when the Space Shuttle is fully operational. And they learned too that men can live and work in weightless conditions almost indefinitely, but only if they devote a great deal of time—around two hours per day—to taking exercise. Because the Sun was very active at that period, sending out lots of solar flares which had the effect of making Earth's atmosphere thicker, Skylab began slowing much earlier than expected, and fell back to Earth in July 1979. Parts of it were so heavy that several tonnes did not burn up, and chunks of metal fell in the Australian outback. NASA, worried that some of it might fall on cities or houses, had made special emergency preparations; but happily no one was hurt. Future American space stations will have guidance engines like Russia's, to make sure they fall harmlessly into the sea.

Apollo–Soyuz   The last time America used the famous Saturn rocket and Apollo spacecraft was in 1975, when after years of discussion and preparation, Russia and America finally made a joint flight. America built a special Docking Module, which was carried into orbit on the Saturn rocket in the same way that the Lunar Module had been sent up for the Moonflights. On July 15 the Russians sent up a two-man Soyuz from Baikonur, commanded by Alexei Leonov (the man who made Russia's first spacewalk) with Valeri Kubasov as his Flight Engineer, making his second flight. Then, $7\frac{1}{2}$ hours later, the Americans launched an Apollo craft from Cape Canaveral; it was commanded by Tom Stafford, making his fourth flight; the Docking Module Pilot was Donald Slayton, the only one of the original Mercury 7 astronauts who had never flown (because the space doctors had been worried about his heart); and Vance Brand, also making his first flight. Soyuz waited in orbit until Apollo found her and docked 52 hours later. There was great excitement when the crews opened their docking hatches, and Stafford and Leonov leaned through for the first Soviet–American space handshake. For nearly 48 hours the two crews exchanged visits, entertained each other to meals, and exchanged flags, medals and souvenirs. There were congratulatory talks—televised for all the world to watch—with the Soviet and US Presidents.

The two crews also did some important experiments, processing metals from both countries in the Multipurpose Furnace carried in the Docking Module. Then the two craft undocked and carried on with their national programmes; Soyuz came home after six days, Apollo after nine days. The home-coming of the Apollo crew was not a happy one. Because they forgot to operate the Earth Landing System Switch, poisonous gas from the Reaction Control System thrusters was sucked inside the spacecraft. Stafford, Slayton and Brand got through the usual brassband welcome on the aircraft carrier which picked them up in the Pacific Ocean, but the gas had burned their lungs. They had to spend two weeks, mostly in hospital, in Honolulu, before being allowed to return to their homes in Houston. But apart from that, the first international spaceflight was considered a great success, and is likely to lead to America's Space Shuttle docking with a Soviet space station in the 1980s. It also led to much other collaboration—especially in 1978, when 10 Soviet and American spacecraft all arrived at Venus within three weeks in December; the two countries helped one another to collect the data and pictures from each other's spacecraft.

Soyuz 19, photographed by Apollo crew during the joint Apollo-Soyuz flight in 1975

(below)   How Apollo astronauts and Soviet cosmonauts met and shook hands in space (artist's concept)

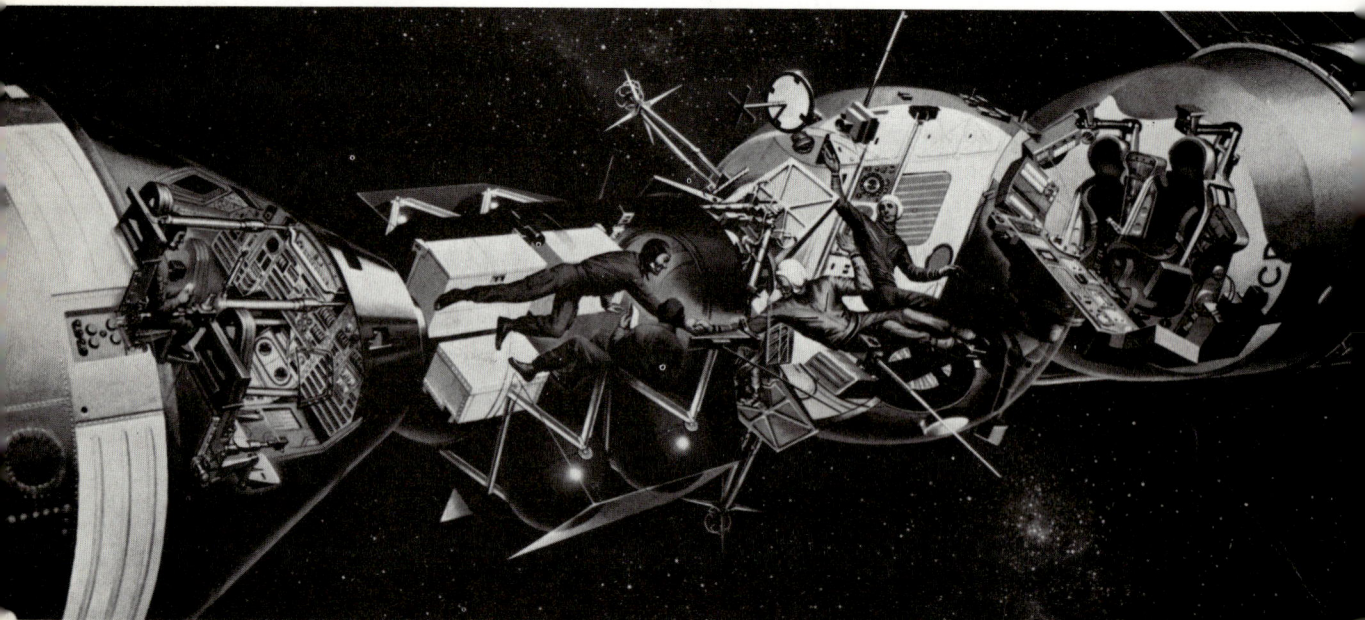

CHAPTER FIVE

HOW SPACE TRAVEL STARTED

Section 18   Spaceflight Dreams

No one knows who first thought of spaceflight, but men have dreamed about it for centuries. The dreams began when early man first realized that there were other worlds besides our own. Probably the astronomers of ancient Egypt and Greece, studying the movements of stars in relation to our own Sun and Planets, were the first to realize that. And of course on clear nights the Moon always seems temptingly close.

Probably the first fictional story about a journey to the Moon was written about AD 100 by Lucian of Samos. But for nearly 2000 years after that, man had to make do with dreams and stories. By the mid 1800s, however, stories by people like the famous French writer, Jules Verne, talked of using rockets for flights to the Moon. One of Verne's stories even began with a launch from Florida in the United States, not far from where the Apollo flights actually began almost exactly 100 years later. That was not just a coincidence; by that time the astronomers had worked out that by starting spaceflights near the equator, and launching in an easterly direction, they could give the rocket a 'free lift' of about 1600 kph since that is the speed and direction at which the Earth itself revolves. Science fiction writers like Verne and H G Wells became so knowledgeable about astronautics, and the problems of overcoming gravity and being weightless in flight, that their ideas about how to overcome these problems helped the scientists a great deal as they searched for practical solutions.

When one remembers that, to get into Earth orbit, a rocket must accelerate to a speed of 8 km per second, or over 28,000 kph, one wonders how the men in the 1800s could ever have thought that people would find a way to do it. Not even the motor car had been invented then, and the fastest people could travel was by the newly invented steam engine. Speeds of 100 kph were only just within reach. Here are the approximate speeds they actually needed to fulfil their dreams:

Sergei Korolev, seen here talking to Cosmonaut Yuri Gagarin, the world's first man in space. Korolev, a brilliant engineer, led the design and development of Russia's rockets and spacecraft, from Vostok right up to Soyuz and Salyut, until his death in 1966. Until then his name was a closely guarded secret. Much to his resentment, he was allowed to be known only as 'The Chief Designer'. He did much of his work during eight years in a scientist's prison during Stalin's cruel reign. The technical setbacks that delayed development of Soyuz and Salyut for several years were almost certainly the result of Korolev's early death at 59

LAUNCH SPEEDS REQUIRED

Mission	kph
Earth Orbit	28,000
Moon	40,000
Mars or Venus	42,000
Jupiter	51,500
Pluto	56,000
Nearest Star	59,500
The Sun	112,600

In our lifetime Sergei Korolev and Wernher von Braun determined to make those dreams come true—and they did.

It took 400,000 scientists and technicians, working at aerospace factories and NASA centres all over the United States, to send the first men to the Moon. Among them, German-born Dr Wernher von Braun will always be remembered, since it was he who led the design and development team which produced the giant Saturn 5 rockets which sent them there. Von Braun's remarkable career began in 1930, when he was 18, with rocket experiments for the German Society of Space Travel. During World War II, he was at Germany's Peenemunde Rocket Centre, and designed the V2 rockets used to bombard Britain and Holland in 1945. He surrendered to the US Army, went to America, and became an American citizen. It was his Redstone Rocket, developed from the V2, which sent Alan Shepard and Gus Grissom, the first two Americans in space, on the 15-minute up-

68

and-down flights which preceded Glenn's first orbital flight. He finally fulfilled his lifelong personal dream to send men to the Moon with his Saturn 5, standing 110 m high, weighing 3000 t and able to launch over 45 t to the Moon. He never knew failure: 15 of his Saturn rockets sent 45 men into space without the loss of a single life. When he died in 1977, aged 65, he was working on solar space stations to gather the Sun's energy and beam it back to Earth.

Section 19 *How They Made the Dreams Come True*

Every time you take a step forward, you do it by pushing *backwards* on the opposite leg. That is exactly how a rocket moves forward—by burning fuel inside, and thrusting backwards as the hot gases rush out through its carefully arranged jet nozzles.

Sir Isaac Newton worked out the principles of motion in the 17th Century; and it was his Third Law, that 'every action results in an equal and opposite *re*action' that enabled mathematicians and engineers of later centuries to work out how to build space rockets. But of course to force its way upwards, through the Earth's atmosphere, a rocket must also overcome gravity—and Sir Isaac Newton worked out the laws of gravity as well. All bodies, he pointed out, from the largest star in the universe to the smallest particle of matter, attract each other with what is called a gravitational pull. The closer two bodies are to each other, the greater is their mutual attraction. The amount of 'pull' on a man or any other object at the Earth's surface is known as one gravity, or '1G'; and when a man or spacecraft is weightless in space, that is called Zero-G, or 0g.

So, to leave Earth on space missions, the launch rocket must accelerate to the right speed to overcome the pull of Earth's gravity. 'Orbital velocity', or 28,300 kph, as mentioned above, is the speed needed to place the Space Shuttle in orbit at a height of 215 km. At that height and speed, the downward pull of Earth's gravity is exactly balanced by the Shuttle's forward motion; the vehicle will be in a state of 'continuous fall', its path exactly matching the curve of the Earth.

It will continue to go round and round *almost* indefinitely; but not quite. At very low orbits like that, there is still enough atmosphere to create some drag on the spacecraft and slow it down so that it gradually sinks back towards Earth. If it had no engines, a spacecraft would fall back into the atmosphere from a height of only 200 km in just a few days. This is known

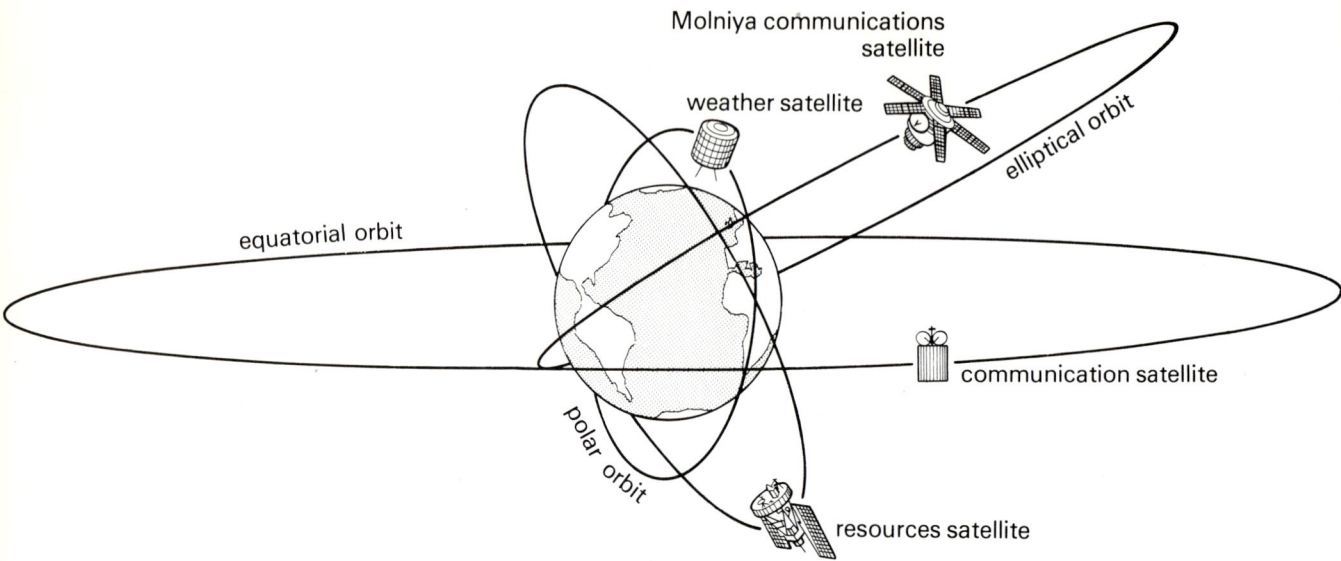

Molniya communications
satellite

weather satellite

elliptical orbit

equatorial orbit

communication satellite

polar orbit

resources satellite

Types of orbit   Polar orbits for military and weather satellites; equatorial orbits for communications satellites; inclined and elliptical orbits for resources satellites

as 'orbital decay'. All orbits decay in time, but the higher you go, the slower they decay.

In low orbits, therefore, which are used for instance by Russia's Salyut space stations, the vehicle must periodically fire its rocket engines to increase its speed and thus raise its orbit once more. But if you start by placing your spacecraft in an orbit several thousand kilometres high, it will stay there for thousands of years.

The reason why the Russians do not do that in the first place is that, with the space stations in a low orbit, they can be more easily reached by heavily loaded Soyuz ferries. Obviously, if you are sending large weights to very great heights (like the Moon or the planets) you need much bigger and more powerful launch rockets.

Section 20   How Rockets Work

Rockets—or as NASA prefers to call them, Launch Vehicles—burn a chemical fuel, which is either liquid or solid. Fireworks use solid fuel, like gunpowder, but until recently this was difficult to control. So, until the end of Apollo the Americans always used liquid-fuelled rockets for manned spaceflight, because liquid fuels, though still difficult, are safer and easier

70

to handle than solid fuels. Now that methods have improved, however, the Space Shuttle is being launched with a combination of both liquid-fuelled and solid-fuelled rockets.

A 'cut-away' view of the giant Saturn 5 liquid-fuelled rocket which sent men to the Moon is a good way to see how rockets work. Bear in mind that an aircraft jet engine, which also works by reaction (thrusting backwards to push itself forwards), uses oxygen from the atmosphere to burn its fuel. Rockets, which pass quickly through the atmosphere into space must carry their own oxygen with them to mix with their fuel and make it burn.

The Saturn 5 was in three stages, or sections. The reason for this was that, to lift its 3000t launch weight, enormous quantities of fuel were needed to get it started—15 t per second. But by dropping off successive sections as the fuel was burnt off, the amount of weight to be lifted was quickly reduced so the upper stages had less to do.

In the 1st Stage, Saturn's lowest tank contained 940,500 l of kerosine (much the same as paraffin used for home heating). In the tank above that was 1,505,200 l of liquid oxygen. (By making it very cold, oxygen which is normally a gas, turns into a liquid and takes up far less space.) The kerosine and oxygen were fed into the five 1st Stage engines, and when burnt the hot gases rushed downwards through the nozzles and gave an upward 'reaction' or thrust of 3,375,000 kg. With the four outer nozzles being automatically swivelled by computers to keep the vehicle on course, the 1st Stage lifted the vehicle to a height of 61 km and a speed of 8530 kph in only 2½ minutes. Then it fell away and dropped into the sea and the 2nd Stage engines started up.

In that section the bottom tank carried 373,500 l of liquid oxygen and the upper tank 1,170,000 l of liquid hydrogen. That provided six minutes of 'burn time', during which the 2nd Stage engines raised the vehicle's height to 183.5 km and the speed to 24,625 kph. Then that too fell away, and the 3rd Stage took over.

The job of the 3rd Stage was quite different. Again it had liquid oxygen (90,670 l) in the lower tank and liquid hydrogen (312,750 l) in the upper tank. Its first job was to take over from the 2nd Stage, and fire for 2.75 minutes to place itself and the Apollo spacecraft in an Earth 'parking' orbit at 28,000 kph. Then, after the three astronauts on board had checked all the systems, it was fired again for over five minutes to increase the speed to 39,270 kph, thus starting Apollo on its journey to the Moon. Soon after that, the Apollo spacecraft separated, turned around, docked with the other end of the 3rd Stage, and drew out the Lunar Module which had until then been carried safely inside the 3rd Stage. After that, Apollo and the Lunar Module went on together to the Moon, and the 3rd Stage was fired yet again so that it crashed on the Moon as part of the scientific experiments. Apollo's Service Module was really a 4th Stage rocket, for manoeuvres around the Moon.

Saturn 5 cutaway

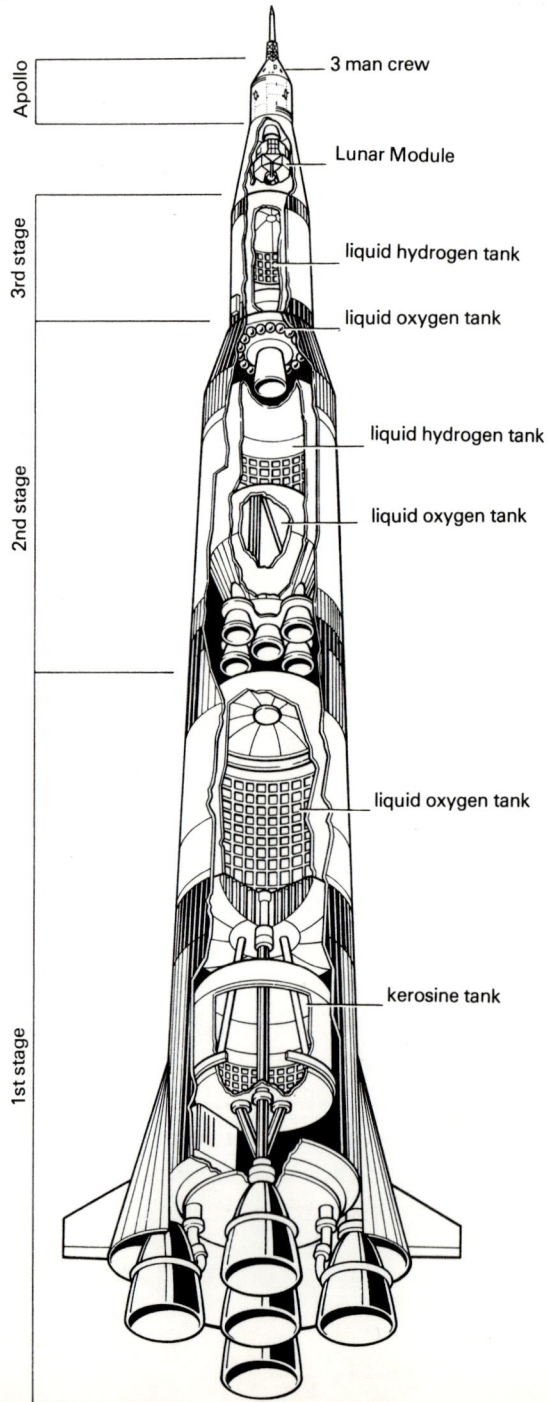

Apollo

3 man crew

Lunar Module

3rd stage

liquid hydrogen tank

liquid oxygen tank

liquid hydrogen tank

2nd stage

liquid oxygen tank

liquid oxygen tank

kerosine tank

1st stage

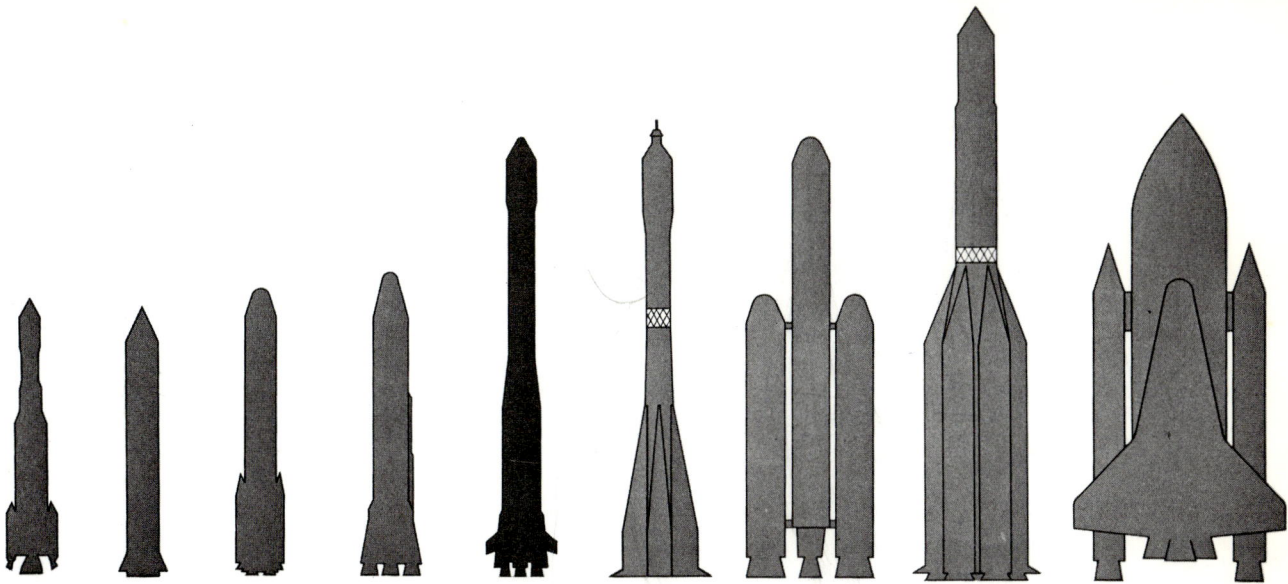

ROCKETS FOR THE EIGHTIES

	N	C-1	Delta	Atlas-	Ariane	A-2	Titan	D-1e	Space
		Cosmos	3914	Centaur		Soyuz	3-C	Zond	Shuttle
	(Japan)	(USSR)	(USA)	(USA)	(ESA)	(USSR)	(USA)	(USSR)	(USA)
1	400	700	2500	6500	4500	7500	15,000	22,000	30,000
2	250	350	900	1850	1700	2400	4500	5000	— *
3	130	150	440	910	925	1100	1500	1600	— *

1   *Payload weight (kg) which can be placed in low Earth orbit*
2   *Payload weight (kg) which can be placed in geostationary transfer orbit*
3   *Payload weight (kg) when geostationary orbit is reached*
*   *Depends on use of Upper Stage or Space Tug*

Section 21 *Rockets in the Eighties*

When America's five Space Shuttles are fully operational, they will make most of America's famous launch rockets—Delta, Atlas and Titan 3—unnecessary and out of date. By the mid 1980s all of America's satellites, both civil and military (including the famous 'spy' satellites) will be taken into orbit by the Shuttle. And NASA is hoping that the rest of the Western world will help to fund the system by paying them to launch their satellites as well. They will probably succeed in this; for although Europe and Japan are making launch rockets of their own, so that they are not completely dependent upon America, the European Space Agency's Ariane rocket and Japan's 'N' rockets are not likely to be used for more

Europe's new satellite launcher being prepared for the first firing on the equatorial launch site at Kourou, French Guiana

than 3 to 4 launches each per year. So far Russia's efforts to build a rocket as big as the Saturn 5 have been unsuccessful and several have blown up in massive explosions. She is still believed to be working on it, however, though it would seem more practical now to follow America's lead in switching to a re-usable Shuttle system.

CHAPTER SIX

EXPLORING THE SOLAR SYSTEM

Section 22   The Search for Other Worlds

We are certain now that Earth's people are the most advanced creatures of our Solar System. Nowhere on the nine Planets and their 34 Moons circling the star which happens to be our Sun, is there any life more advanced than ours. Even though it may be another 50 to 100 years before manned expeditions visit all the planets and their moons, we already have the ability to communicate with them all. So if any other body in the Solar System contains a more advanced civilization than ours, we can safely assume they would have communicated with us. There may of course be some developing forms of life—perhaps even primitive manlike creatures—on some of the moons of the Outer Planets. But so far we have found no evidence of any life-forms at all on the Inner Planets, and we know that conditions are not suitable for us to live on Mercury, Mars or Venus. The likelihood of finding any congenial companions on the moons of the gaseous Outer Planets like Jupiter, Saturn, Uranus and Neptune is equally remote.

In the last 20 years, man has learned an astonishing amount about the Solar System—far more than all the astronomers, no matter how clever, have been able to discover in the previous 2000 years of studying the sky. These discoveries have been made by eight spacecraft sent out to study the Sun; over 50 sent out to the planets by America and Russia, and over 100 (nine of them manned) sent to the Moon. The Inner Planets—so called because they are nearest to the Sun—have already been fairly thoroughly mapped and studied by the sensors and cameras of unmanned spacecraft. Now the Outer Planets are being explored. And by the time this book appears, America's Pioneer 11 spacecraft should have sent back man's first close-up colour pictures of Saturn and its rings, and of its huge moon Titan. This chapter summarizes recent discoveries, starting at the centre of that tiny part of the Universe which we call our Solar System. (See also Chapter 7 which deals with Earth Satellites.)

Section 23   The Sun

Our Sun, quite a small star compared with the billions of other stars in the Milky Way, controls the movements of the nine planets with its gravitational pull—so great, that if a man could stand on the Sun's surface he would weigh 2 t. Since 1962 eight spacecraft called Orbiting Solar Observatories have made many discoveries about the Sun, which is 149.6M km from Earth, and has been likened to a very slow-burning hydrogen bomb. The OSO spacecraft, and 75,000 solar pictures taken by the Skylab astronauts in 1973, led to many new discoveries about the 11-year period during which solar activity gradually rises to a peak and then subsides again. They found that some solar flares—violent explosions which send out energy and material—have temperatures of over 30M°C. A single flare can release as much energy as the whole Earth uses in 100,000 years. They also discovered 'holes' in the Sun's corona, where temperatures are much lower than on the rest of the Sun. It is from these 'holes' that the so-called 'solar wind' (a supersonic stream of particles) streams out into space. Some scientists think the Sun will continue to keep

(left)   Skylab astronauts took this picture of a solar eruption on June 10 1973. An occulting disc blocks out the Sun itself, and on the left can be seen the swirling eruption expanding into space at a speed of 1.5M kph. When such eruptions are towards Earth they cause magnetic storms, displays of auroras (better known as the Northern and Southern Lights), and even cause radio blackouts. Activities like this also affect Earth's atmosphere, and it was just such activity that caused Skylab itself to slow down and fall back to Earth much sooner than originally expected

OSO-7 OBSERVATIONS

Orbiting Solar Observatory
No 7 (superimposed upper
left) took this picture of the
Sun hurling out three gas
clouds (left centre) in
1971. Total mass ejected
was 20 times the size of
Earth. Energy generated
would have met Earth's
electricity needs for one
million years !

COOL POLAR CORONA

VISIBLE CORONAL
STREAMERS

EJECTED ION CLOUDS

X RAY PICTURE OF SUN

(below)   One of two Solar
Polar Spacecraft drawing
near the Sun to study its
polar regions for the first
time

THE SOLAR POLAR MISSION

OUT-OF-ECLIPTIC ORBIT

"LAUNCH AT EARTH"

JUPITER SWING-BY

Solar Polar Trajectories   This picture shows how the two unmanned Solar spacecraft, after being launched by the Shuttle, will fly out to Jupiter and use the giant planet's gravity to hurl them in opposite directions around the Sun's poles. In the background are shown the orbits of Earth and the other Inner Planets

us warm for another 5 billion years, but since man's survival depends upon it, we need to know a lot more about the way the Sun works. So one of NASA's most important 1979 launches was the Solar Maximum Mission which will watch solar flares during 1980–81, because that is the peak of the present 11-year solar cycle. And in 1983 NASA and the European Space Agency plan to send up a pair of spacecraft to study the Sun's north and south poles, which are cooler than the rest of the Sun, and have very big 'holes'. Because all the Planets orbit the Sun's equator it is very difficult to put spacecraft in polar orbit around the Sun ('out of ecliptic', it is called); they must first be sent around Jupiter, and use Jovian gravity to fling them into Solar Polar Orbit—hence it is called the Solar Polar Mission.

Section 24   Mercury

Little was known about our smallest planet Mercury, which orbits between 46M km and 70M km from the Sun, until the Mariner 10

78

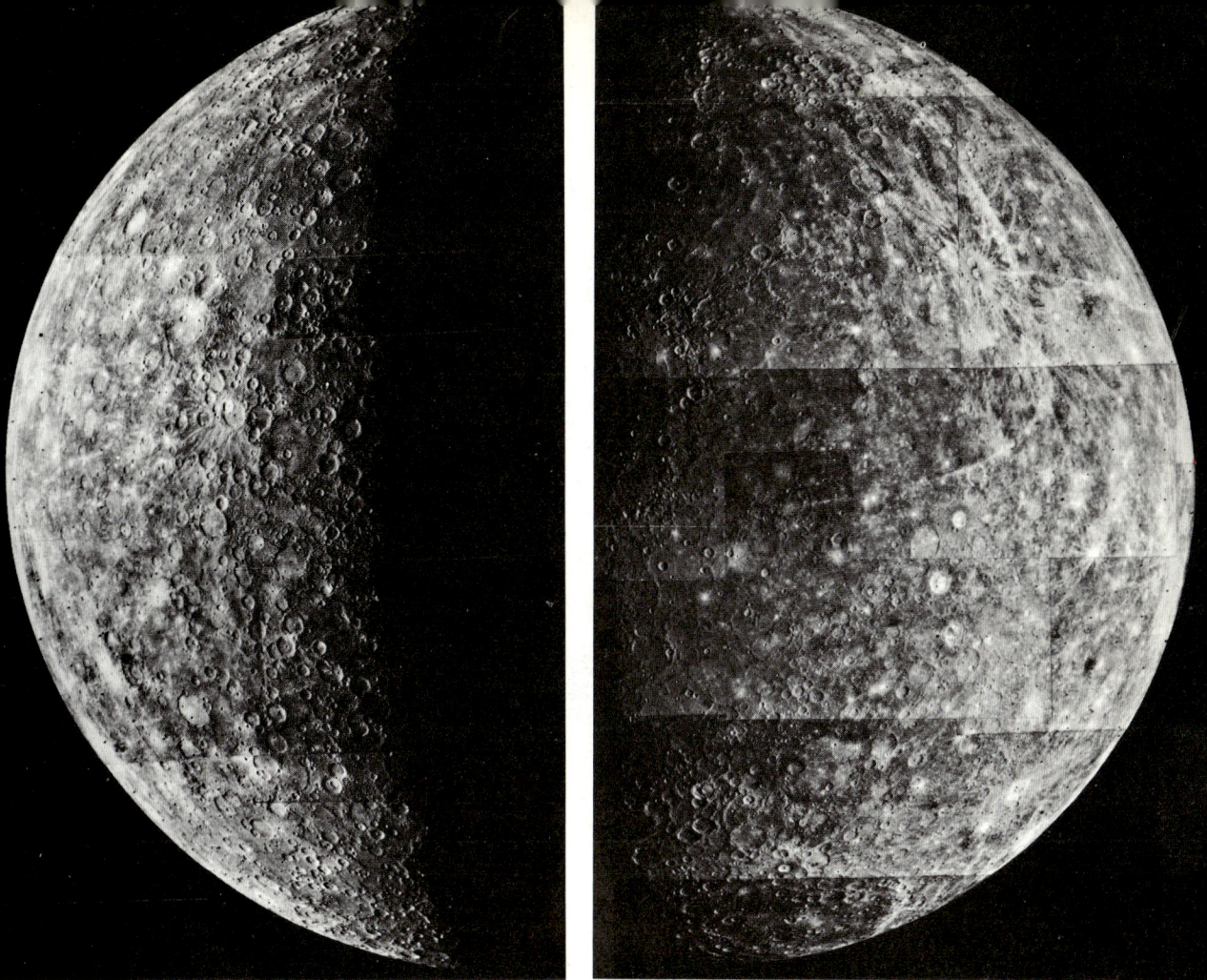

These two pictures are photomosaics—each consisting of 18 photos taken at 42-second intervals as Mariner 10 flew past Mercury at a distance of about 200,000 km. The biggest craters are 200 km in diameter; note the bright 'rays' extending for enormous distances from the craters

spacecraft flew past it three times in 1974. Astronomers had always found it difficult to study through their telescopes because it was so near to the Sun. Now, from 10,000 highly detailed pictures sent back by Mariner, some from only 431 km away, we have a Mercury atlas—not quite complete because one side was in darkness during the spacecraft's passes. Astronomers were astonished to find that Mercury, though far from the asteroid belt, had been just as heavily bombarded by meteors as the Moon, and has many enormous craters. One of them, Caloris, is 1280 km across, and the collision that made it was so severe that the surface on Mercury's opposite side was shattered too. But though Mercury is like the Moon on the outside, it is more like Earth inside, with a large heavy core of iron.

MARINER VENUS – MERCURY FLIGHT PATH

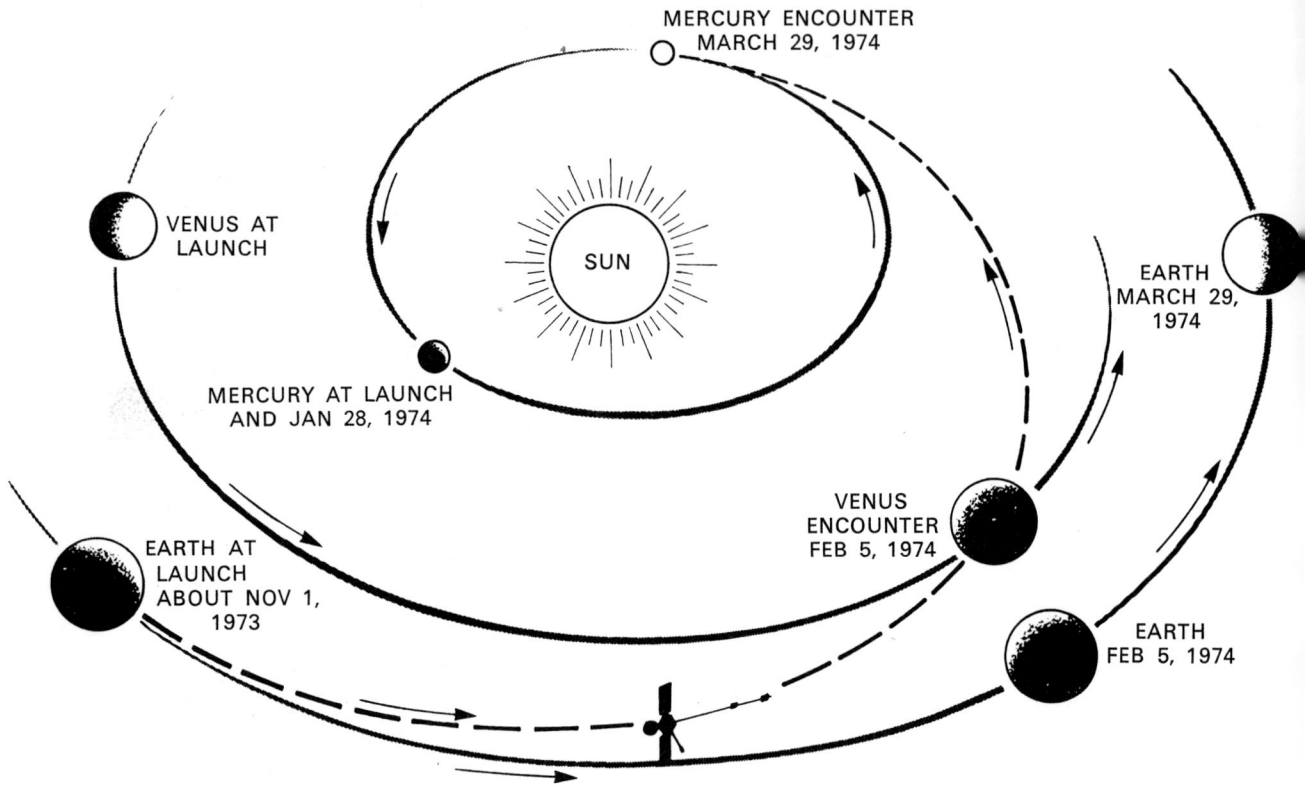

MERCURY ENCOUNTER
MARCH 29, 1974

VENUS AT
LAUNCH

SUN

EARTH
MARCH 29,
1974

MERCURY AT LAUNCH
AND JAN 28, 1974

VENUS
ENCOUNTER
FEB 5, 1974

EARTH AT
LAUNCH
ABOUT NOV 1,
1973

EARTH
FEB 5, 1974

This diagram shows how Mariner 10 was launched from Earth so that it gradually caught up with Venus. Then having photographed that, it went on to take pictures of Mercury

Mercury's 'day' is equal to 175 Earth days; one-third the size of Earth, with almost no atmosphere, it can never have supported any form of life.

Section 25 *Venus*

By the end of 1978 29 spacecraft—23 of them Russian—had been launched towards Venus. After 14 years of persistent work, and many disappointments, Russian scientists were rewarded in October 1975 when their Venus 10 and 11 spacecraft survived just long enough in 460°C temperature and air pressure 100 times that of Earth's to send back the first surface pictures. The big surprise, since confirmed by later Soviet and American spacecraft, was that Venus had a solid, very rocky surface, and there was plenty of light (rather like a cloudy summer day) below the

Mariner 10 took this picture of Venus's thick clouds as it passed on its way to Mercury

three thick layers of cloud. These clouds, starting at about 49 km above the surface, and extending to 63 km, contain sulphuric acid particles, and whirl around at 320 kph. Russia and America are continuing to study Venus with some anxiety, because the 'greenhouse' effect, in which the Sun's heat is trapped below the cloud layers, thus heating up the surface, could just possibly happen on Earth too if we do not take care not to pollute our atmosphere. America's two 1978 Pioneer Venus spacecraft, one placed in orbit and the other carrying five probes to study the atmosphere, is to be followed in 1983 by an Orbiting Radar Mapper, able to 'look' through the clouds and map the surface. Venus is the second nearest planet to the Sun and slightly smaller than Earth; it reflects so much sunlight from its dense clouds that on clear nights it is so bright as it appears just above the horizon that it often starts 'UFO' scares.

At last we are penetrating the mystery of what the Venusian surface is like. These pictures show how the radar spacecraft will, figuratively speaking, 'peel away' the clouds as it looks through them and map the surface in great detail

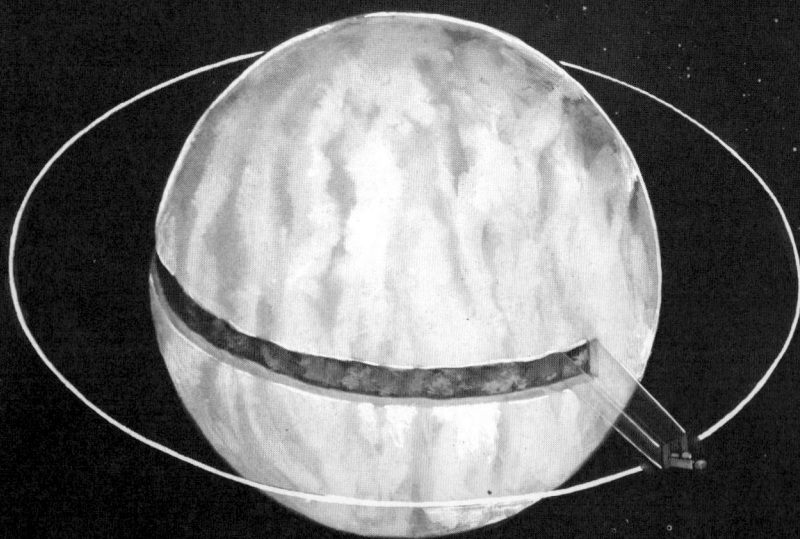

Section 26 Earth's Moon

What do we know about the Earth's Moon that we didn't know before the six successful Apollo Moonlandings between 1969–72? Most important, examination of the 385 kg of lunar rock and soil brought back by the astronauts has shown that a solar furnace could extract water, oxygen and hydrogen from it. So it *is* possible for man to establish bases on the Moon, and to support himself there. We know that the core of the Moon is hot, not cold as many astronomers believed. The amount of heat escaping from its interior is much higher than expected—about half that of Earth. We still don't know whether the Moon is made of material which was once thrown out from the Earth's equator; or whether it was once an independent body in solar orbit which was captured by Earth's gravity. Because the Moon's composition is different from Earth's, the second theory is more likely; perhaps the Earth captured a whole series of small asteroids, which were thrown together to make up the present Moon. There are still many mysterious features of the Moon which remain

Scientist-astronaut Harrison Schmitt, who is now a US Senator, examining a bus-sized boulder amid the Taurus Mountains during Apollo 17, the last Moonlanding. By then he was breaking off pieces as big as a football to bring home

unexplored because the Apollo crews did not have enough manoeuvring fuel to enable them to risk landing near the much more rugged lunar poles. Nor, of course, could they land on the Moon's farside, though they photographed and studied it in great detail from lunar orbit. Russia, America and the European Space Agency are talking about possible joint missions to the Moon; a spacecraft placed in polar orbit around the Moon, instead of the equatorial orbits which was all that the Apollo craft could manage, could find out many new things.

Section 27 Mars

The Red Planet, half the size of Earth, was called Mars by the Romans after their god of war because of its blood-red hue. Since 1960 22 spacecraft have been launched towards it. The most successful, America's two Vikings, sent down unmanned landers in 1976, and they analysed soil samples in a vain search for signs of life on opposite sides of the planet. But they sent back marvellous colour pictures of the red, rubbly surface, and of the pink sky. The very reverse of Venus, Mars has an atmosphere only 100th as dense as Earth's. But despite that, it often has violent sandstorms

One of Mars' giant
volcanoes, with a
cloud plume of water
ice flowing from it,
was photographed by
the Viking 2 Orbiter

(left) This
Martian landscape
was sent back by
America's Viking 2
Lander on
September 14
1976. It is
remarkably similar to
deserts in Mexico
and California

covering most of the globe. The two Orbiters sent back pictures for more than a Martian year (687 Earth days), covering all the seasons, first from 1500 km, and then from only 300 km. These showed how the carbon dioxide ice caps at the North and South Poles melted during the summer, revealing water ice beneath and frost at the edges. There were dramatic pictures too of Mars' four giant volcanoes; but the landing spacecraft recorded only one Marsquake, showing that Mars is not nearly so active internally as Earth. Perhaps even more exciting were the close-up pictures of the two tiny Martian moons, Phobos and Deimos. Viking 2 passed within 25 km of Deimos. These battered, potato-like objects are heavily cratered; only 19 and 10 km in diameter, it was found that their composition was quite different from Mars itself. Scientists think they may have formed somewhere else in the solar system, and been 'captured' from the asteroid belt by Martian gravity. NASA is anxious to continue searching Mars, to find out for instance whether there was once life which has now died out. Projects—not yet approved—include launching a robot lander which would bring back soil samples; a robot vehicle which could travel about for a year, sending back pictures and information; a U2-like aircraft to survey Mars' 'Grand Canyon'; and a ball, with retractable

Phobos, the tiny Martian moon which is only 21 × 19 km in size, as seen from a distance of 480 km by Viking Orbiter 1

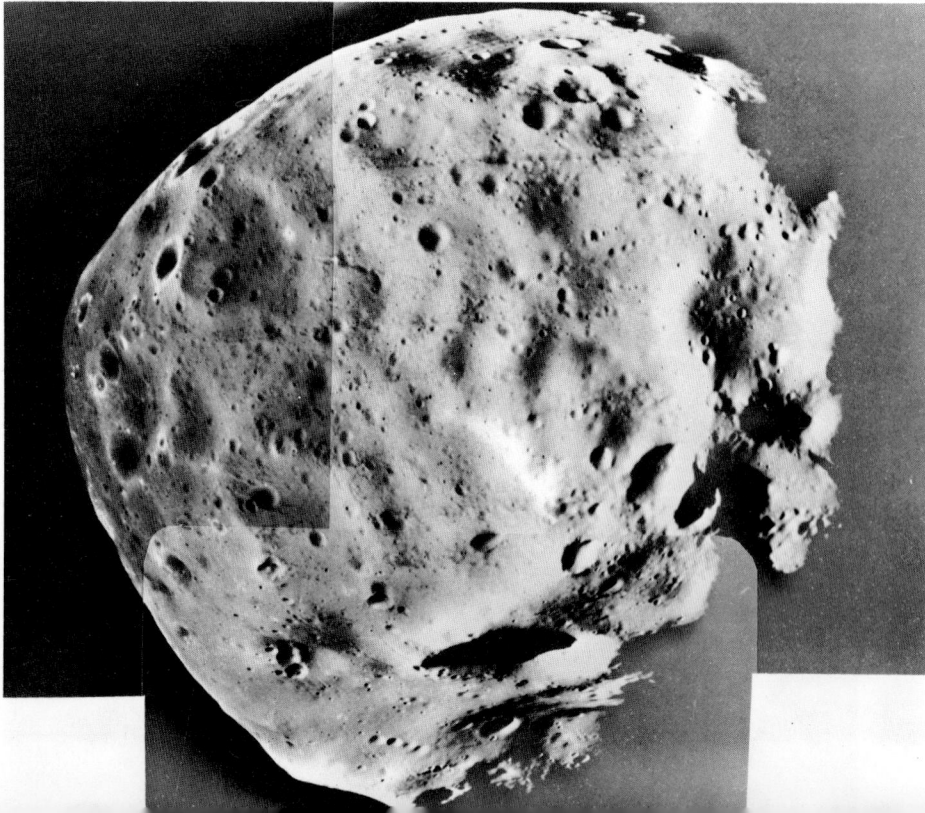

Artist's conception of how the Viking spacecraft landed on Mars. Parachute in background lowered Viking to 6.7 km before being detached

cameras and instruments, which would be blown about the surface by the dust storms and thus cover a large area at minimum cost. At one time there were hopes that there might be a manned expedition to Mars about 1984. Two spacecraft, each carrying about 12 men and women astronauts, were proposed. They would be away for about two years. But so far no one has been prepared to meet the cost, which would be several times the $24M spent by the US on the Moonlandings.

Section 28   Asteroids and Comets

NASA is now making plans to send spacecraft to explore the Asteroid Belt. This consists of perhaps 50,000 mini-planets and large rocks orbiting the Sun between Mars and Jupiter at distances ranging between 300–545M km from the Sun. At one time it was thought it would not be safe to send spacecraft through the belt; but Pioneers 10 and 11 in 1973 and Voyagers 1 and 2 in 1979 passed safely through on their way to Jupiter and Saturn. All the asteroids put together would only make a planet a fraction the size of Earth. The largest, Ceres, is 955 km in diameter; most are tiny battered objects like the Martian moons, because they often collide. Meteors, or 'shooting stars', which can often be seen burning up in

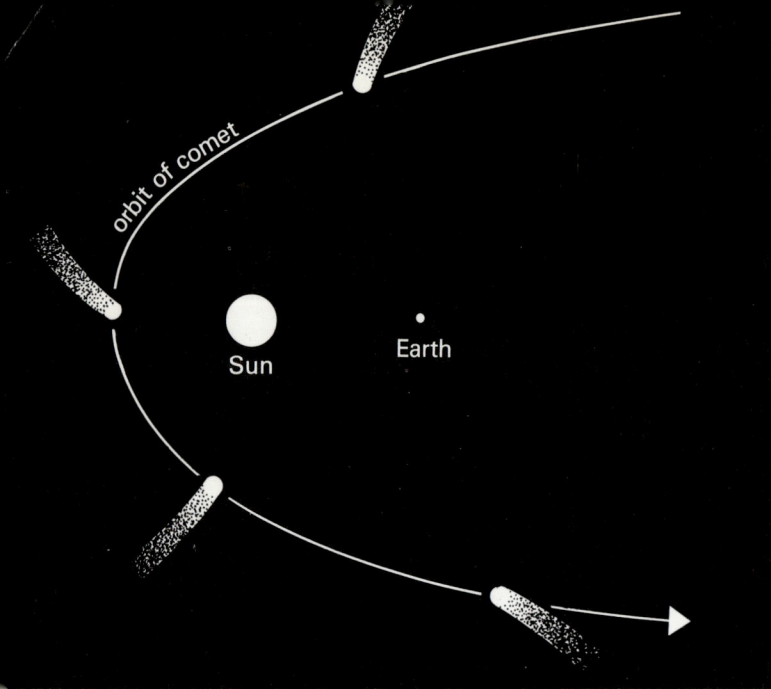

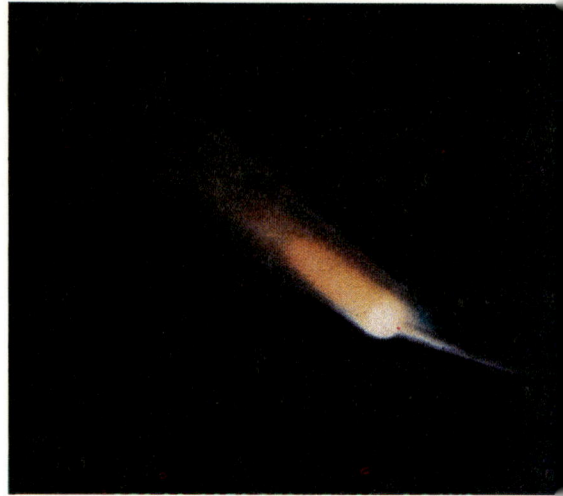

(left)   As a comet passes around the Sun, its tail swings around, so that it departs tail first—the effect of the Sun's heat. Some comets, like Halley's, are in huge elliptical orbits around the Sun, and so regularly reappear. Others, in hyperbolic orbits, head into space after going around the Sun, never to reappear

(right)   Comet Kohoutek as seen by Skylab astronauts in December 1973, two days after passing around the Sun

Earth's atmosphere, are probably fragments thrown out of orbit by these collisions. The reason why NASA—and probably the Russians too—want to examine the asteroids more closely is that they are a valuable source of materials for man-made colonies. Some consist of material like nickel, and it would be possible to attach low-powered ion engines to some of them, and let them make their way into Earth orbit, over a period of say five years. There they could be mined for use in building space colonies—and even provide temporary bases for spacemen during the work.

NASA is also making plans for spacecraft to intercept and examine some comets—the mysterious long-tailed objects composed largely of ice and dust, which regularly pass the Earth as they whirl around the Sun. Comets, it is thought, may be made of the original material from which the planets were formed. A close look at some of them might help solve the mystery of how the Solar System began. NASA is developing a new electric propulsion engine—known as 'ion drive'—for a spacecraft which they hope to send off to rendezvous with the famous Halley's Comet when it passes round the Sun in 1986. Astronomers have watched and recorded it 30 times since 467 BC.

Section 29   Jupiter

Many of Jupiter's secrets have been revealed by four American spacecraft which flew past the Sun's biggest planet, and through its system of 14 moons. They were Pioneers 10 and 11 in 1973/74, and Voyagers 1 and 2 in 1979. Five times further from the Sun than Earth, Jupiter is composed largely of hydrogen and helium gas, and though it takes nearly 12 Earth years to orbit the Sun once, it whirls around so fast that a day is less than 10 hours long. The Pioneers solved the centuries-old mystery of the Great Red Spot, which had puzzled astronomers for centuries because it moves and changes size. It is in fact a continuous hurricane—a mass of whirling cloud 2000 km wide and about 8 km higher than the surrounding clouds. Analysis of Jupiter's coloured cloudbanks suggests it is just possible there

Voyager 1 took this picture of Jupiter on March 4 1979. The great red spot is upper centre. The ring, drawn by an artist, is believed to be 30 km thick and 128,000 km from Jupiter

IO

EUROPA

GANYMEDE

CALLISTO

Voyager 1's pictures of Jupiter's four big satellites. They are all very different. Io is believed to be covered with sulphur and salt, Europa with water ice, Ganymede has both ice and rock and Callisto is mostly rock-covered ice

might be some form of life floating in the third cloud layer about 20 km deep, because this consists of liquid water droplets suspended in hydrogen-helium. Below that, temperatures and pressures become far too great; Jupiter's surface is believed to be hotter than the Sun's. Jupiter's four largest moons—known as the Galilean moons after the man who discovered them in 1610—are the most interesting. Callisto, as big as the planet Mercury, and 1.8M km from Jupiter, has some atmosphere and water, and is the most likely place for a landing by the first spacemen to reach the Jovian system. Ganymede, which is even bigger, and 1M km from Jupiter, is rocky and probably covered with ice; Europa, the same

Callisto appears in more detail in this mosaic of pictures taken from a distance of 202,000 km. Heavily cratered like our Moon, it is Jupiter's most suitable moon for manned landing

size as Earth's Moon, is also believed to have water ice. Io, the orange-coloured moon 421,000 km away, provided the big surprise when Voyager 1 sent back detailed pictures in March 1979. At least six volcanoes could be seen in a continuous state of eruption—the first time *live* volcanoes had been found anywhere other than on Earth. Because Jupiter radiates $2\frac{1}{2}$ times more heat than it receives from the Sun, some scientists regard it as more of a star than a planet, making it a mini solar-system within our own Solar System. And yet another surprise is that Jupiter too has a very thin ring around it, probably of boulder-sized debris, which is not visible from Earth.

Voyager photographed this enormous volcanic explosion as it passed Io; it was one of seven. The material is being thrown up more than 150 km. It was the first time volcanic activity had been observed on another planet

The bright areas on Europa are probably ice. The mysterious straight lines, some over 1000 km long, may be fractures caused by 'tectonic plate' movement

Ganymede, one-and-a-half times as big as our Moon, seen from a distance of 2.6M km

Section 30   Saturn

Saturn, the second largest of our planets, was reached by an unmanned spacecraft on September 1 1979. After a 3.2B km journey lasting 6½ years, Pioneer 11 passed within 20,800 km of Saturn's cloud tops. Pioneer's TV pictures were not so good as hoped, but it made some major new discoveries, despite being hit by two meteoroids as it passed above the rings and three more as it dipped beneath them. It found two more rings outside the three known ones, all probably made of water ice. Saturn's solid centre of iron and rock, twice Earth's size, is so tightly compressed it contains 11 times as much material as Earth. Outside the core there is liquid metallic hydrogen which does not exist on Earth. Pioneer discovered Saturn has an 11th moon, about 400 km in diameter. But Titan, Saturn's largest moon, which has an atmosphere and was thought to be the one place left in our Solar System where advanced life was possible, is so cold that life is unlikely though it cannot be ruled out. The Voyager spacecraft, with better cameras than Pioneer, reach Saturn in 1980/1; then we should learn more about this planet which spins so rapidly that its day lasts only

93

Photographs of Saturn and Earth are shown here to the same scale, so that their sizes may be compared

This is how the two Voyager spacecraft, which have already sent back pictures of Jupiter, will arrive at Saturn in November 1980 and August 1981

10 hours, but which is so far from the Sun – 1727M km – that a Saturnian year lasts 29½ Earth years.

Section 31   *Uranus, Neptune, Pluto*

So far, the three outermost planets, Uranus, Neptune and Pluto, have only been studied with Earth-based equipment; but bigger telescopes, radio antennas and powerful radar systems are slowly unravelling their secrets. It was only in 1977 that a group of observers watching a star passing behind Uranus discovered that that, like Saturn, had a series of rings around it, in addition to its five moons. Smaller and colder than Jupiter and Saturn, Uranus and Neptune are still much larger than Earth, and very similar to one another, with gaseous atmospheres and solid cores. It is hoped that Voyager 2 will still be working after examining Saturn, so that it can be sent on to study Uranus in January 1986, and Neptune in September 1989—12 years after being launched, and 4.5 billion km from the Sun. Pluto, the last of the nine planets so far discovered, is more like the Inner Planets in size and composition. Some astronomers think it is not a true planet at all, but an 'escaped' moon of Neptune having been thrown into a very strange orbit around the Sun after nearly colliding with Triton, the largest of Neptune's other two moons.

Uranus, it is hoped, will be inspected by Voyager 2 in January 1986, over eight years after the spacecraft's launch. Uranus is now believed to have nine rings

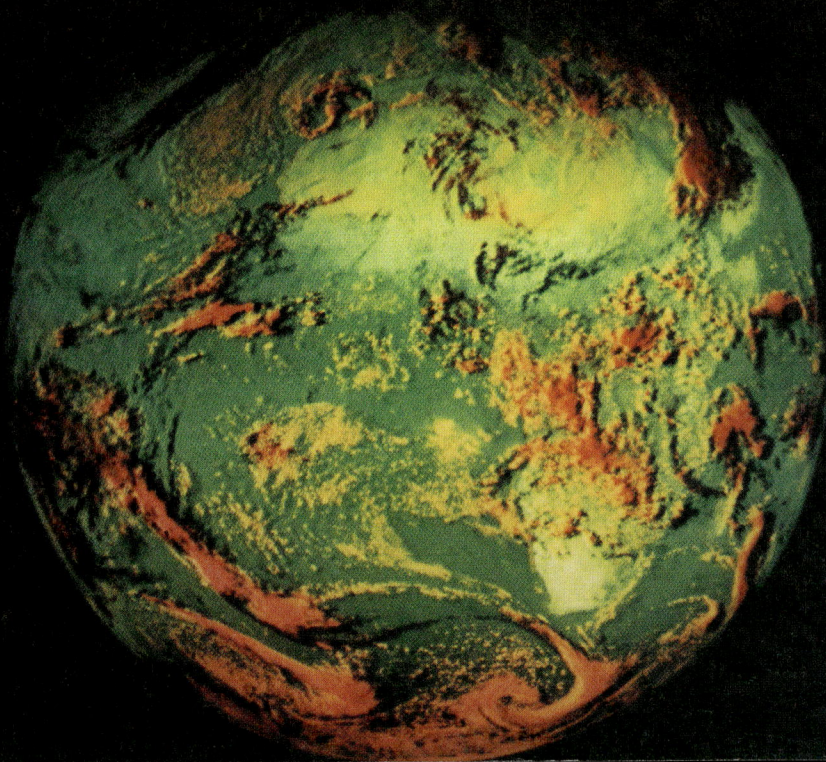

Every 30 minutes
Europe's Meteosat
sends pictures like
this—a visible image
(top), and an infra-
red image (bottom)
of Earth.
Meteorologists use
them around the
world, and praise
their high quality
and detail. Meteosat
also sends other
pictures showing the
amount of water
vapour in Earth's
atmosphere at any
given time—the first
satellite with this
capability

CHAPTER SEVEN

ROBOTS IN SPACE: What They've Done

Section 32   Space Benefits for Everyone

Everyone's life, in every country, has been changed by the space age. And despite many criticisms that the vast amounts spent on spaceflight have been of little benefit to ordinary people, examination of the facts shows that this is just not true. The most obvious example of benefits in developed countries is the daily TV satellite transmissions around the world, which enable ordinary people to see and understand what is taking place as it happens, no matter how far away: whether it is a war or a football match, live and recorded pictures of it are bounced via 'stationary' satellites for immediate use. Medical benefits are astonishingly wide-ranging: heart-pacemakers developed from NASA's miniaturized power systems (more than 100,000 people per year are being fitted with them) and voice-controlled wheelchairs, developed from remote-controlled switches for astronauts, are two examples. New methods of testing blood, and of taking X-rays of soft parts of the body as well as of bones, are others.

By the end of 1978 a total of over 2500 unmanned satellites had been launched. Many were 'spy satellites' which are dealt with in Chapter 9; but nearly 650 of them had been placed in a great variety of orbits around the Earth, providing communications, helping our ships to navigate, giving warning of storms and hurricanes, and using all sorts of sensors and infra-red techniques to study Earth's resources, including its fish stocks and agricultural potential.

This chapter gives some examples.

Section 33   Satellites on Weather Watch

Since 1966 weather satellites have given warning of every major storm system as it built up at any point on the globe. Not one has been missed. While we can't yet change the weather, or prevent the storms (though

Before the space age this child would have died. Her life was saved by fitting her with a heart pacemaker developed from NASA's miniaturized power systems. She is seen here being given her weekly battery re-charge, without pain and with little inconvenience

plans to do so are described under the 'Spacelab' section), these early warnings that storms are on the way have already saved more than 100,000 lives in the United States alone. Weather forecasters around the world have been relying for many years past on the continuous stream of weather pictures sent back by America's Tiros, Nimbus and NOAA satellites. Starting on December 1 1978, 145 countries joined in a programme organized by the World Meteorological Organization to study the world's weather over a one-year period. It is called GARP (Global Atmospheric Research Programme). America's GOES-1 and GOES-2 satellites, Europe's Meteosat satellite, and Japan's GMS satellite have been placed at intervals in 'stationary' orbits around the equator, so that between them they can watch and photograph the whole globe in great detail.

In addition America's Nimbus-7 satellite was sent into polar orbit with delicate sensors which it is hoped will find out whether Earth is warming up or cooling down. Measurements of the atmosphere and the seas are being made at the same time, to find out how seriously man is polluting the air by burning so much oil and coal, and the sea by pouring sewage and waste chemicals into it. For their regular daily forecasts, Britain's weathermen use satellite pictures sent back by America's NOAA-5 satellite, which are received by a specially built station at Dundee University. There was a big disappointment for them in October 1978, when Seasat-1, a new type of satellite intended to sweep across 95% of the world's oceans every 36 hours and keep the forecasters supplied with details of wave-heights, ocean currents, surface winds, and drifting ice, stopped working after only 106 days.

98

Section 34   Spaceguards for Crops

From their 900km orbits Landsat satellites are able to measure crop yields around the world, so that shortages and gluts can be forecast and avoided; they map mountain snows so that the amount of 'run off' for irrigation and providing electric power is known in advance. They give warning of lakes and seas being polluted by sewage and oil. Dr James Fletcher, a previous head of NASA, said if he had to pick one space age development to save the world, it would be Landsat, and there seems no reason to dispute his choice. Since 1972 three Landsats have been launched, with a fourth due in 1981. As new techniques are developed, each has more advanced 'remote sensors', able to detect things that the human eye cannot see. All objects—people, plants, rocks—transmit or reflect light and heat in a slightly different way, and so have their own 'signature' or 'fingerprint'.

Landsat's polar orbits are carefully arranged to be 'Sun synchronous'; that is, as they go round Earth from north to south, two of them can use their sensors and cameras to study any spot every nine days with the Sun in exactly the same position. That means the Sun is always lighting up that spot from the same angle, and changes can easily be detected. Landsats don't send back photographs, but 'images'. Data is transmitted at the rate

How Landsats work

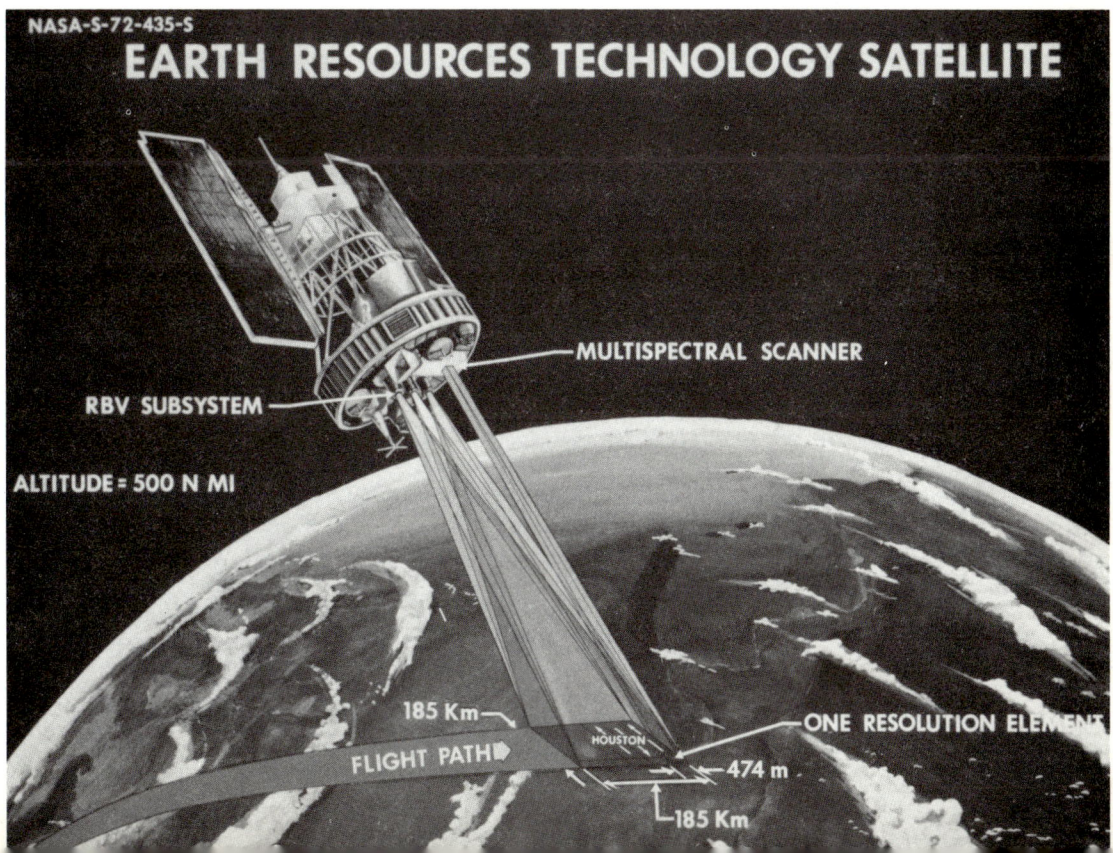

NASA-S-72-435-S

EARTH RESOURCES TECHNOLOGY SATELLITE

MULTISPECTRAL SCANNER

RBV SUBSYSTEM

ALTITUDE = 500 N MI

185 Km

FLIGHT PATH

HOUSTON

ONE RESOLUTION ELEMENT

474 m

185 Km

(above left) Landsat picture of
Dead Sea area shows the Jordan
River with Jerusalem and
Bethlehem at right centre. Healthy
crops, trees and other green plants
show up on the infra-red pictures as
bright red, barren lands as light
grey, with clear water completely
black. Diseased crops show up in
different colours

(above) This mosaic of Italy was
built up from 46 Landsat pictures
taken when each area was cloud free

(left) Lageos, intended to help
predict earthquakes, should stay in
orbit for over 8 million years

of *15 million* 'bits' per second to computers, which convert the data into images on photographic film. Slightly different colours—64 levels of brightness—show whether crops and forests are healthy, or are developing blight or disease, so that it can be treated before it gets worse. In 1978 a three-year experiment was completed to see whether Landsats could be used to forecast the size of the world's most important grain crop, wheat. Landsat's multispectral scanners estimated that Russia's wheat crop would be 91.4M t—less than 1% below the official Soviet figure of 92M t. So in future it will be much more difficult for countries like Russia to do what they have done in the past—quietly buy up other nations' wheat crops at low prices before the outside world knows that their own crop has failed. Anyone, in any country, is allowed to buy Landsat pictures for their own use; America now has a stock of over 6,000,000! Many countries, including Brazil, Italy and Canada, Argentina, Chile, India, Zaïre, Australia, Japan and Sweden, have either built or are planning their own ground-receiving stations so that they can receive their own Landsat images direct. They pay America $200,000 per year for the service.

Section 35   *Earthquake Imminent!*

Only in the last few years has it been established that the Earth's crust is divided into 'plates', the size of continents. There are about 12, and some

The lines on this map show the edges of the 'tectonic plates' on the Earth's crust, where earthquakes are likely to occur

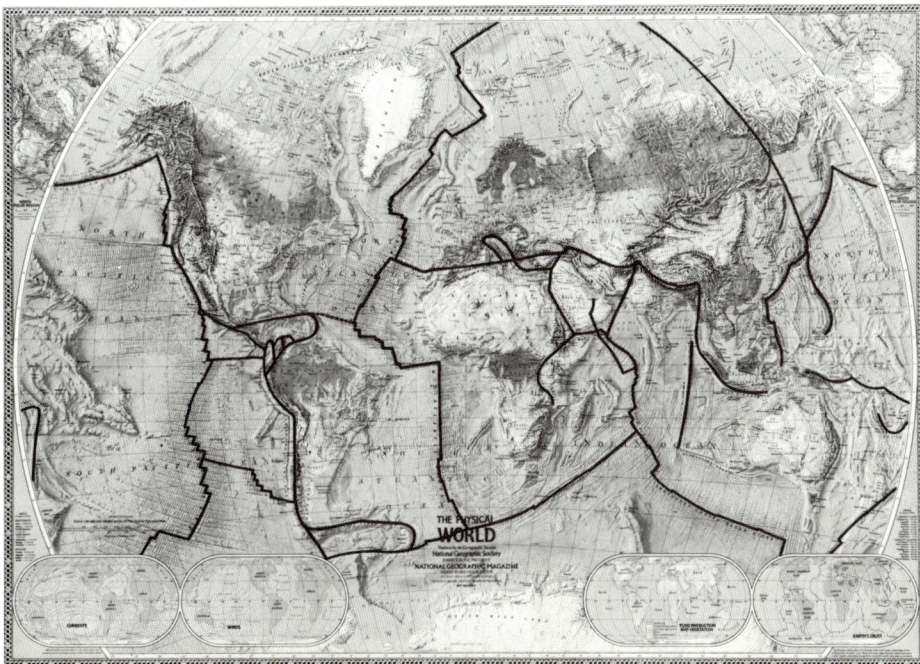

are gradually moving apart, while others are sliding against each other, and causing earthquakes. Having discovered what causes them, the next step is to learn how to predict when serious quakes are likely, so that people living in the area can be given advance warning. To do this, NASA has sent up LAGEOS, which stands for Laser Geodynamics Satellite, to a height of 5900 km. It is a very solid aluminium sphere with a brass core; it has 426 prisms set in it, so that it looks like a very large golf ball. Laser beams fired at it from Earth are reflected back by the prisms so accurately that geologists expect to be able to track movements on the Earth's surface as small as 2 cm. It will take some years to perfect the system; but already they have been able to establish that two points 900 km apart on each side of the famous San Andreas fault in California are moving together at a rate of 6 to 12 cm per year. The beautiful city of San Francisco stands on the San Andreas fault, and lives in fear that one day there will be a repetition of the earthquake which destroyed large parts of it in 1906.

Section 36   The Communications Explosion

The first live TV pictures, bounced across the Atlantic by the Telstar 1 satellite on July 23 1962, were a sensation. Despite being divided by more than 3000 km of sea, people in Europe and the United States now had a 'window' through which they could see and talk to one another. Telstar, the first privately owned satellite, was built for the America Telephone and Telegraph Company, and was soon making money from TV companies with live pictures of America's astronauts conquering space during their Mercury and Gemini flights. But the drawback with these early TV satellites was that since they went round the Earth in fairly low orbits (about 6000 km), they were only available to receive and transmit pictures for about an hour at a time before disappearing below the horizon. The answer to this problem had been suggested by space writer Arthur C Clarke long before in 1945—that satellites orbiting at a height of 35,680 km would exactly match the speed of the Earth's rotation, and thus remain all the time over the same spot. These 'synchronous', or 'stationary', satellites would always be in position to relay radio, TV and telephone signals, and no elaborate tracking devices would be needed to keep ground transmitters and receivers moving in line with them. And by 1964 the first truly synchronous satellite, Syncom 3, had been manoeuvred above the equator over the Pacific Ocean in time to telecast the Tokyo Olympic

The latest Intelsat 5 satellites can handle 12,000 telephone calls at once

Games. By 1979 Intelsat—the International Telecommunications Satellite Consortium—was providing a global communications service for over 100 countries. Usually about seven operational satellites are hovering at various points around the equator. The Intelsat 4As now in service can each carry over 6000 telephone calls and two TV programmes; the latest Intelsat 5s will have double that capacity, and will work for at least seven years before they must be replaced. Direct dialling via satellites has increased the number of transoceanic phone calls from 3M in 1965 to an estimated 200M in 1980. And this is only the start of the communications explosion. The famous Wall Street Journal is now being sent from New York, a page at a time (each page takes $3\frac{1}{2}$ minutes) by satellite to Florida, so that thousands of copies can be printed simultaneously there; people in that area can thus buy the newspaper much sooner, and without having to pay heavy airmail charges.

The next step being planned is an electronic mail service. Starting with business letters, these will be fed into computers every evening and satellited to their destinations. Offices thousands of miles away will find

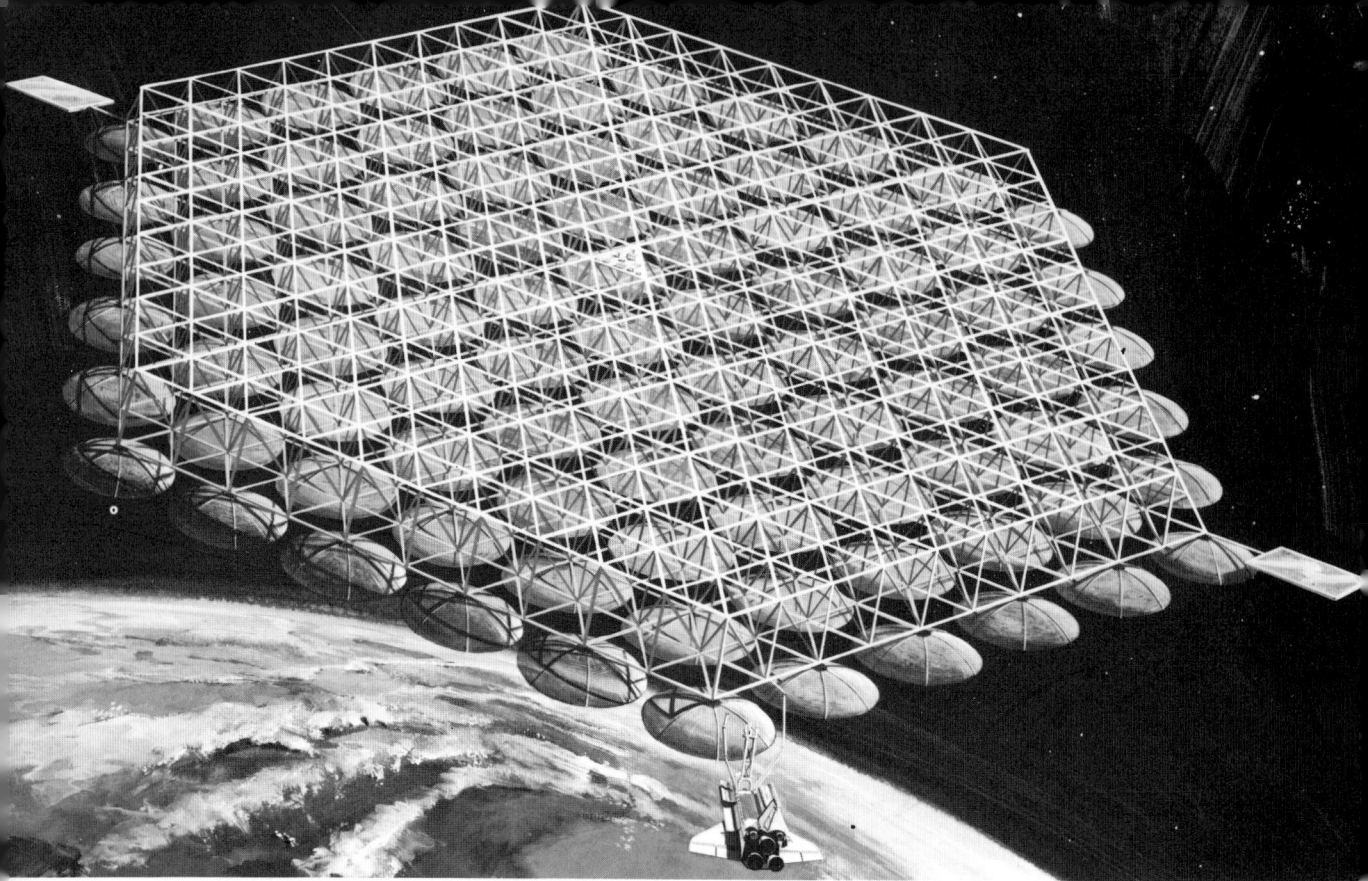

Electronic Mail   This space platform, 300 m across, will transmit photographic copies of letters and other documents between countries and continents. By using word-processing machines, they can be sent from one office to another, thousands of miles apart, in a few minutes

them printed out on their computers first thing in the morning. The world's Post Offices are already working out how to provide an electronic mail service for private letters too. To get the cost down, the letters will be transmitted at night when the satellites are not so heavily used; here again, it will be possible for a letter posted in London at night to be delivered first post next morning to an address in Australia or Japan.

Section 37   Education by Satellite

The world's first educational satellite ATS-6 (standing for Applications Technology Satellite No. 6) was designed and launched 'to bring the benefits of space technology to backward areas by lessening ignorance and poverty'. It succeeded in a remarkable way. Launched in 1974 for a

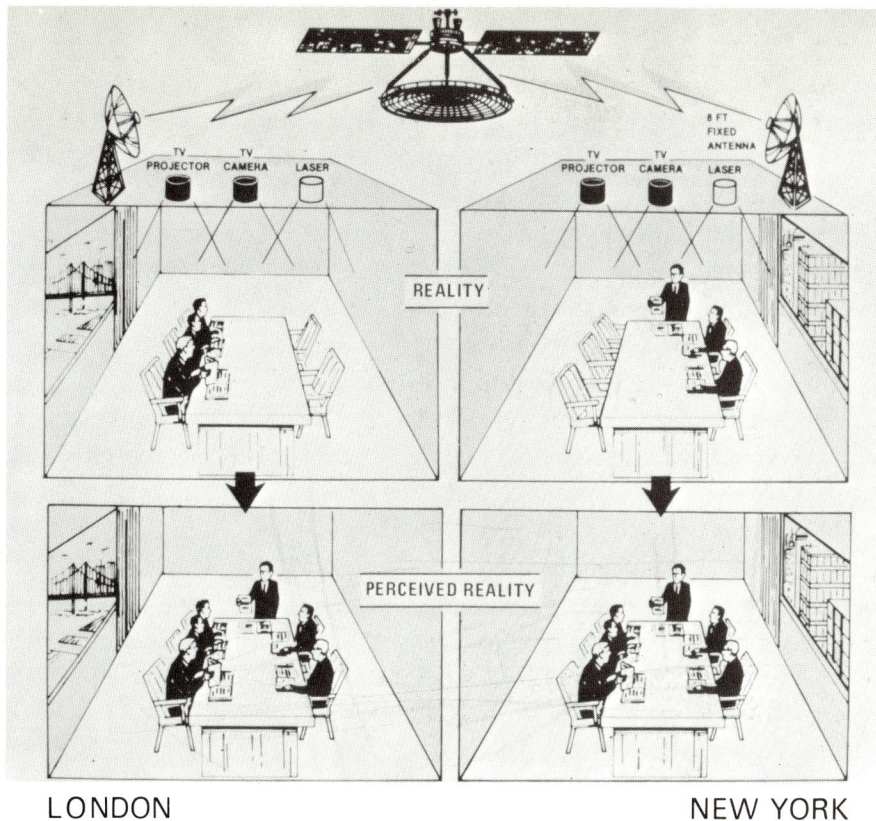

LONDON   NEW YORK

These pictures show how TV images can be transmitted between conference rooms, say in New York and London, so that busy executives and technicians need not travel to meet one another. The same people appear to be in both places at once by means of what are called 'holographic techniques'. Almost the only thing they can't do is to shake hands!

planned two-year mission, it was expected to continue operating until 1981. A powerful TV transmitter, two storeys high, and radiating 200,000W of effective radio-energy (compared with Intelsat 4's 6400W), ATS-6 was first placed in synchronous orbit over the Galapagos Islands in the Pacific. From there it spent a year beaming special courses to students in remote schools in the Rocky Mountains, and at the same time provided a two-way medical service for sparsely populated Alaska. Doctors were able to *see* people who had been injured thousands of miles away, and advise on their treatment. Then its educational activities were transferred to India, by arrangement with the Indian Government. ATS-6's on-board rocket motor was fired to move the spacecraft 12,800 km along the equator. It was 6 weeks before it was halted again above Lake Victoria in East Africa. From there educational transmissions were sent direct to 2400 Indian villages. About 5 million people, living in the most primitive conditions, many of whom had never even heard of television, were fascinated. It had taken months to equip each village with a TV set and erect very simple 3m diameter antennas made of chicken wire, which could receive the programmes. They gave the children a new interest in education; in lessons prepared by the Indian Government they learned simple things like how to make toothbrushes (which few had ever owned) from thin tree-branches; and to improve health and hygiene by moving open-air washing places away from the community wells. The men were taught better ways of farming; Indian mothers were taught that it was bad to breast-feed their babies until the age of 3; it was better to start feeding them with solid food much earlier. And the lessons suggested solid foods that were available in their areas.

It was a sad day for the villages when the year was up and ATS-6 was moved back for more work in the United States, on the way doing similar demonstrations over 30 African countries. But the Indian Government was so impressed that they have ordered their own Direct Broadcast Satellite from NASA. It is to be launched by the Space Shuttle early in

(right)   Residents of an Indian village watching a TV programme. The simple chicken-wire antenna in the background is receiving the picture and sound direct from ATS-6, 35,600 km above

(below)   ATS-6, with a 9m reflector antenna, is one of the most powerful spacecraft yet launched

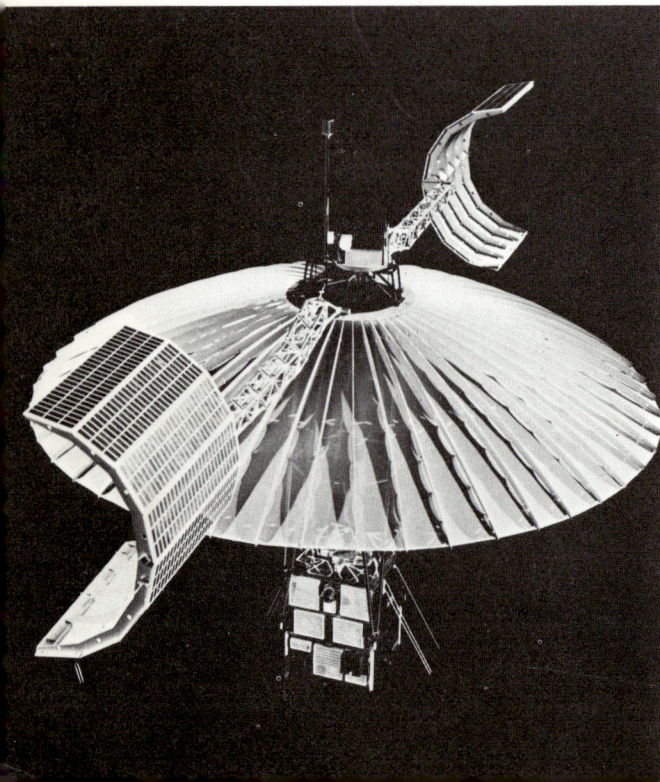

1981, and soon after that a growing number of Indian villages should have a permanent TV service.

Some nations, however, are getting very worried about Direct Broadcasting Satellites—DSBs as they are becoming known. Just as many countries now use radio for propaganda purposes, so within a few years it will be possible to use DSBs to transmit TV programmes right into the homes of people in other nations. (Though of course, the right sort of aerial, a dish-shaped antenna 0.8 m in diameter, will be necessary to receive the programmes.) Some countries, including the Soviet Union, want a new international agreement to be made, under which no country will be allowed to send TV to another country without the consent of its Government. But others, led by the United States, insist that nothing should be done to restrict the free flow of information, and the freedom of ordinary people to exchange ideas and knowledge.

Section 38   Space Spinoff

Who would have thought that space technology could help to solve some of our sewage problems? Some extraordinary 'spinoff' benefits have resulted from NASA's policy of asking employees at their space centres to suggest ways of using their discoveries to improve everyday life. At NASA's Space Technology Laboratories in Mississippi it was noticed that water hyacinths, for long regarded as pernicious weeds which grew so rapidly that they clogged rivers and streams, in fact purified the water in which they grew. Their experiments have shown that if water hyacinths are grown in lagoons into which raw sewage is fed, they rapidly absorb the pollutants, so that fresh water flows out at the other end; better still, water hyacinths grow so rapidly that they can be cropped, dried, and used as fertilizer, or for feeding cattle, or even as a fuel.

In another case an engineer testing materials for insulating a lightweight rocket motor, was looking for a substance from which to make carbon. He discovered that sewage solids provide an excellent raw material—and then found that the activated carbon he produced was ideal for treating sewage. As a result a pilot plant was built in California in which filtered solid sewage is burnt to make activated carbon, and the carbon in turn is used to filter sewage. Handling 4.5M litres a day, the plant is cheaper to operate than conventional sewage farms, and at the end produces water just as clean as other methods.

CHAPTER EIGHT

SPY SATELLITES AND SPACE WAR

Section 39   What It's About

The race between East and West to be first in space started soon after the last war ended. Both sides feared that whoever was first to develop military spacecraft would dominate the world and be able to tell other countries what to do under threat of bombardment from space.

Happily, it didn't work out like that at all. Because it was so expensive, Europe soon dropped out of the space race, and left it to America and Russia. And during their race to be first to get men on the Moon (which America finally won on July 20 1969 with the Apollo 11 Moonlanding) they decided it would be wise to make an Outer Space Treaty. Many people, including the author, think that Treaty saved us from a Third World War. Russia and America agreed not to send up any spacecraft carrying nuclear weapons. Even more important, as it turned out, they decided not to object to one another's 'reconnaissance' or spy satellites. What this meant was that both sides were able to monitor the military activities going on in the other side's territory. America for instance believed at one time that Russia had far more ICBMs (Inter Continental Ballistic Missiles), and began spending enormous sums of money to 'catch up'. When their spy satellites found this just was not true, they were able to cut back on military spending. For many years, as the spy satellites kept watch, it enabled both sides to spend much less on the arms race than they would have done if both were worrying about getting left behind.

Nowadays then, spy satellites—and there are many different sorts—can watch everything that goes on anywhere in the world, no matter how remote the place may be. Russia sends up 80 to 100 military satellites every year; America about 10 to 15. Exactly why Russia needs so many more than America, no one in the West fully understands. But although both sides try to keep their military satellites top secret, by careful study of their orbits and what happens to them, Western observers have been able to find out a great deal about them, as this chapter explains.

The real 'spy' satellites are in very low Earth orbits, taking photographs and 'listening in' to what is going on; but many others, much more sophisticated and in much higher orbits, are there to keep watch and give

Night launch by Titan 3 of America's top-secret Big Bird spy satellite

'early warning' of any attack by either ICBMs or aircraft; others provide communications and navigation systems for warships, aircraft and armies.

It is these very sophisticated early warning and communication satellites that are the problem now. While both sides are still observing the Outer Space Treaty, the Russians apparently do not think it prohibits them from developing 'killer satellites' able to destroy the early warning satellites. That, combined with the new laser beam systems which can be used to interfere with satellites, are causing worries about the possibility of a Space War which is described in Section 42.

Section 40   What the Americans are Doing

No actual 'spy' pictures have yet been published, but by studying pictures of Earth sent back from 900 km by Landsat satellites, we know that America's 10t Big Bird spy satellites, from the much lower heights of 150–

This Landsat picture of Cape Canaveral, in which every launchpad is clearly visible, indicates how much more detail can be obtained by Big Bird, which flies much lower with much more sophisticated cameras and sensors

250 km, can take even more detailed pictures. Aircraft and tanks, and even the men servicing them, can be photographed in minute detail. Sweeping round every 90 minutes, repeated pictures of launch sites can monitor the progress of launch preparations, count the number of rockets at missile bases, and check whether the number has been increased above the limits agreed between America and Russia under their SALT (Strategic Arms Limitation Treaty) talks. Nowadays, too, both sides watch the oceans. The US Navy has Ocean Survey satellites which can track ships in all weathers, equipped with radio frequency antennas which can 'listen in' to their radar and communications signals. The pattern of such signals provides a clear indication of what sort of activity is going on. The same satellite can even plot the course of submerged missile submarines by detecting the wake of warm water they leave behind after they have used it to cool their nuclear reactors.

As mentioned in the last section, both Russia and America were already designing spy satellites long before Russia launched Sputnik 1 in 1957. They were still not operational at the time America was worrying about Russia's military build-up and the possibility that Russia had far more ICBMs in specially protected missile sites, able to be fired distances of 10,000 km at American cities and bases. That was why America sent her

110

high-level U-2 planes on reconnaissance flights (and military men always prefer to talk about 'reconnaissance' rather than 'spying') over Soviet territory in 1957–60, until Gary Powers was shot down by a Soviet ground-to-air missile in May 1960. There was a fierce political argument between America and Russia about that; but the U-2s had by then found and photographed Russia's Tyuratam missile base and space centre, from which all the manned flights have since been launched. To make it harder to find, the Russians have always called it Baikonur, although it is 375 km away from there. (As time went on, the spy satellites found that Russian maps, as part of Soviet defence policy, deliberately gave inaccurate positions for many places of military importance.)

As a result of the U-2 row, the Americans promised to send no more spy planes over Soviet territory; but there was no need to anyway. After many failures, they were soon launching their Discoverer spy satellites from the secret US Air Force base at Vandenberg in California. They were placed in polar orbits, which meant their cameras could look down at almost all the Earth's surface; they took excellent photographs, which were automatically placed in a re-entry capsule and sent back to Earth. As they came down on parachutes, aircraft tried to 'capture' the capsule by trailing a framework which would catch in the parachute harness. If that failed, ships would be on station to recover the capsule and its precious film package from the sea.

Nearly 20 years later that system is still in use, though TV techniques are now so good that it is no longer so important. The Big Bird spy satellites, built inside upper-stage Agena rockets, are sent up several times a year by the huge Titan 3D rockets. They stay in orbit three to five months; as they begin to fall back to Earth, the Agena engine is fired to raise it again. In addition to sending back film packages about six times, photographs can also be processed on board. They are scanned by a laser device, and the pictures are converted into electronic signals transmitted to US Air Force bases in various parts of the world. This is much quicker than collecting the film packages, but does not show such exact detail.

By 1984 America hopes to complete a Global Positioning System (GPS), which will consist of 24 satellites and have many different uses. The satellites will have atomic clocks, all exactly synchronized, to help them fix any point on Earth or in space with an accuracy of 10 m. Ships, aircraft, and even individual soldiers, will be able to use the system to communicate with one another, and work out exactly where they are themselves, or where the enemy is. The satellites will be able to measure

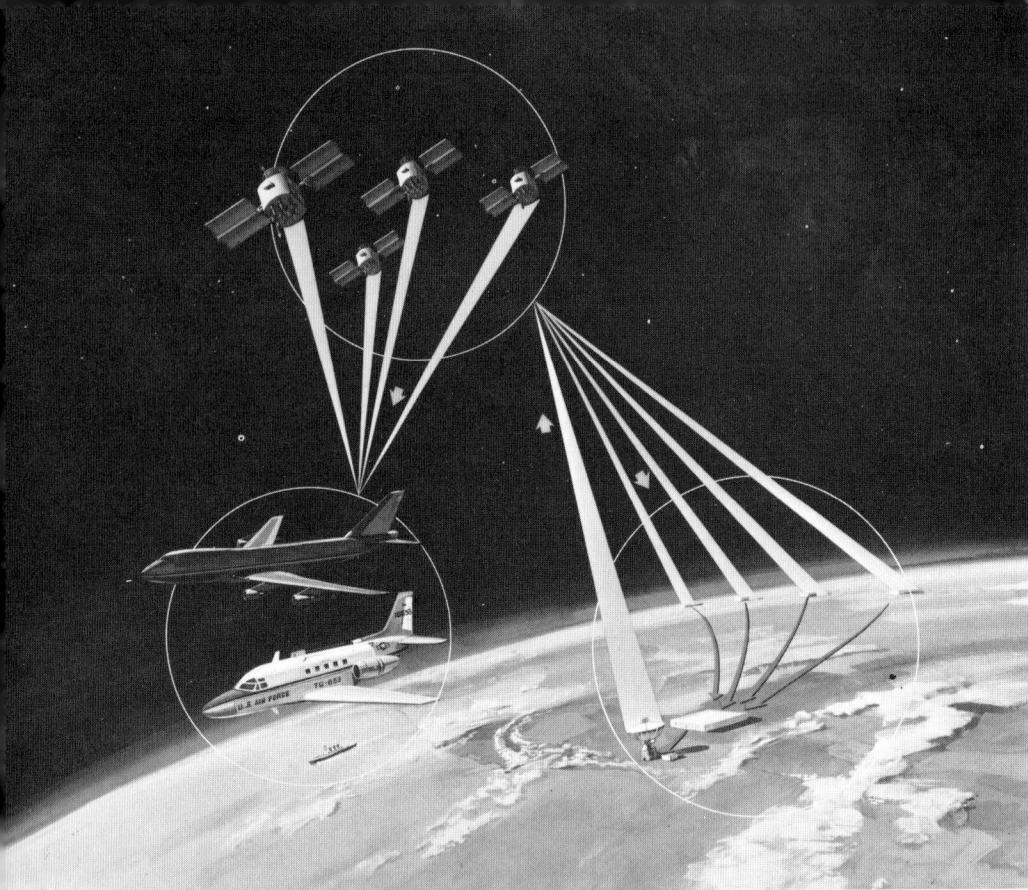

This picture shows how Global Positioning Satellites will link aircraft, ships and ground forces. Instructions and information will be fed into all their computers simultaneously, so that everybody has the latest information at the same time

(left)   This double test-launch of Minuteman missiles from America's Vandenberg missile base in California gives an idea of what a mass launch of such weapons would be like

(below)   NAVSTAR satellites, part of the US Global Positioning System, which enable ships, aircraft and soldiers to check their exact position. Early warning satellites would flash warning of Soviet missiles being launched by detecting their heat within 90 seconds. Russia has even more complicated networks of satellites watching what happens in the West

the course and speed of attacking missiles with an accuracy of 0.03 m per second—very important of course, if you want to intercept and destroy them before they arrive. They will also be able to monitor and correct the course of America's own missiles while they are actually in flight. This system alone is costing $2 billion.

And of course the US Air Force will be using two military versions of the Space Shuttle. This, it is hoped, will compensate for the loss of military bases in countries like Iran. They will use the Shuttle to deliver and service GPS satellites, as well as Early Warning satellites like TRW 647, as shown in Space War on page 115, with its special infra-red telescope able to detect the heat when a missile is launched.

Section 41   What the Russians are Doing

Every two weeks, without fail, the Russians send up a spy satellite, its orbit carefully adjusted so that it can gather pictures of current military interest—for instance of the Chinese invasion of Vietnam in February 1979. The satellite is brought back, with its load of film and tape recordings of radio activity, after 13 or 14 days. In very tense situations it can be brought back earlier. These fortnightly spy satellites often overlap by a day or two; 26 were sent up in 1978.

In addition, four times every year Russia sends up eight small satellites on one rocket. These are to provide direct military communications between ships, planes and Soviet bases. About 24 of these 100cm spheres, each weighing 41 kg, and taking two hours to orbit the globe, are needed to provide continuous 24-hour coverage. But Soviet military chiefs like to

This BMEWS tracker at Fylingdales on the Yorkshire Moors in England would pick up the Soviet missile attack just after the satellites. It would give Britain four minutes' warning and America 15 minutes' warning of their exact targets. Honeycomb pattern in background is the interior of the tracker's golf-ball like protective radome

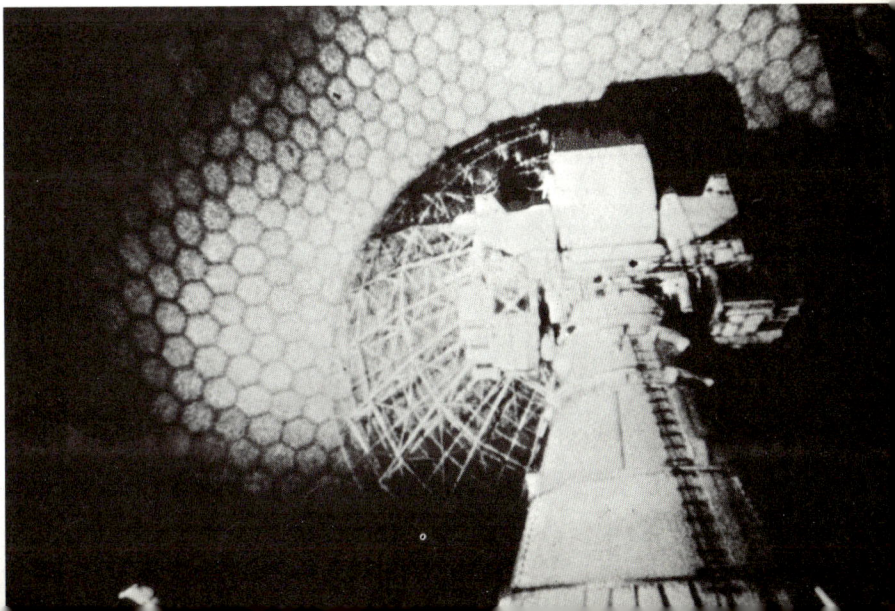

have about 48 always available, so that it would be impossible for the West to jam all of them at the same time. More than 200 of these little communication satellites have been placed in their 1500km orbits since 1970. They are operational for only about two years before their batteries and fuel supplies are exhausted; but since it will be more than 10,000 years before they fall back to Earth, their orbit is becoming increasingly cluttered with dead ironmongery. No doubt future Soviet space shuttles will collect it up and bring it back to Earth.

In 1978 the 28 fortnightly spy satellites, and 32 military communications satellites accounted for 60 Soviet payloads in the famous Cosmos series. But there were 36 more, in addition to their manned Soyuz launches, Meteor weather and Molniya TV and radio satellites. Some were undoubtedly for scientific research; but we just do not know with any certainty what the others were for.

Section 42   What a Space War Would be Like

Some of the Cosmos satellites sent up by Russia have been practice launches of her interceptor, or 'killer' satellites. Rather like a clay pigeon shoot, Russia sends up one as a target, and then another to knock it down before it has completed one orbit. The killer satellite is placed in a slightly lower orbit than the target, so that it circles the Earth more quickly, and can thus catch it up. When it is near enough it blows up, destroying the target as well as itself. But this, of course, is just the start. Interceptors can be used to approach and inspect target satellites, with cameras and sensors, to find out what they are doing and send back pictures and data before a decision is made to destroy the target.

Laser beams, which are very powerful pencil-like beams of light, can also be directed from ground bases at satellites to 'blind' and damage them. American scientists are fairly certain that Russia has interfered with several of their satellites in this way, just as an experiment to see whether it could be done. What happens here is that Early Warning satellites, often in stationary orbits 32,000 km up, have telescopes and sensors which are very sensitive to light and heat—that is how they can detect and give warning of missile and rocket launches. So, of course, it is possible to upset the whole system by deliberately giving them false warnings. The first early warning satellites often gave false alarms when their sensors picked up very bright moonlight, or forest fires in Russia.

114

SCENARIO FOR SPACE WAR

(top left)   Soviet anti-satellite explodes, destroying both itself and US Early Warning Satellite

(top centre)   US Shuttle inspecting Soviet Molniya-type communications satellite being counter-attacked by Soviet Shuttle's laser weapons

(centre right)   US Shuttle astronaut disabling military Salyut space station before it is captured and placed in payload to be taken back to America. Another Soviet Shuttle has taken off from Baikonur, but may not be in time to intercept

(lower right)   US Navy's satellite 'eyes' are being blinded by laser beams fired from Soviet ground bases.

Now their computers are programmed to ignore things like that. Interference with early warning and spy satellites in this way is a breach of the Outer Space Treaty. But Russia considers that killer satellites are necessary for defence reasons, and are therefore not in breach of it. They also fear that America's new Space Shuttle, though primarily intended for civil use by NASA, might also be used as a manned interceptor and killer satellite. Clearly this is possible; it would be surprising if American Defence Department astronauts did not take the opportunity to manoeuvre close enough at least to some of Russia's military satellites to see what they were like—especially the hundreds of 'dead' ones which have not yet decayed. And since one of the most important jobs of the Space Shuttle is to collect damaged and dead US satellites for repair, it would obviously be quite possible for spacewalking astronauts to cut off or retract the antennas and solar panels on a suspect or hostile Soviet satellite, then use the Shuttle's remote-controlled arms to pull it into the Payload Bay, and take it back for detailed examination in the United States. Alternatively, Russian and American spacemen could merely disable one another's spacecraft with on-board laser systems, or even by simply spraying paint on a hostile spacecraft's sensors and cameras.

However, this sort of pin-pricking spacewar could not be carried out without both sides knowing exactly what was going on, since their radar scanners show the exact positions of all satellites, rocket casings and other debris in space at all times; just like radar in an airport control tower, the scanners would show exactly how the target spacecraft was approached and disabled. Serious attacks on spacecraft therefore seem unlikely unless there is a large-scale war. The real worry is that such a war might begin by one side 'blinding' the other side's early warning spacecraft just before making an all-out missile attack, in an effort to destroy them before they have a chance to retaliate.

Section 43   *Spy Satellites as Policemen*

Nowadays Spy Satellites are being used as policemen, as well as for keeping watch on potential enemies. A remarkable example was between December 1977 and April 1978, when two US Navy Ocean Survey Satellites were used to break up a huge drug-smuggling racket. American secret agents in Colombia sent code messages to their bosses that 40 ships were about to leave that country loaded with 522 t of marijuana, the

116

illegal drug obtained by growing certain types of hemp. The Navy satellites, orbiting at 1000 km, were directed to track the ships, day and night, until finally they were met by a fleet of small boats 360 km off the US coast. When those small boats arrived with their illegal cargoes, the crews were astonished to be met and arrested by waiting Coastguard officials. Operation Stopgap, as it was code-named, reduced by one-third the supply of this evil drug into America. Now satellites like Landsat continually watch the crops of hemp in countries like Colombia, and the experts know when it will be ready for harvesting; and the spy satellites then track the ships in case they are carrying marijuana made from the hemp. And not only has drug smuggling been made much harder; satellites are also being used to watch oil tankers and other ships. More than one captain has been prosecuted after a satellite picture has identified his ship as being responsible for causing pollution which is later washed ashore.

Section 44   *Why Are Spacecraft So Different?*

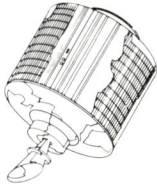

BODY-MOUNTED

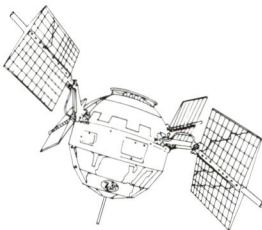

PADDLE MOUNTED

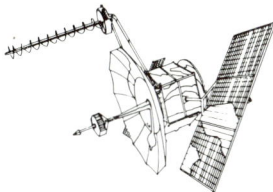

ORIENTED PANEL

The main reason is the different ways they use to gather heat from the Sun to charge their batteries. In these TRW *Quest Magazine* drawings Fig 1 shows a spacecraft with solar arrays mounted all around its body because it is spin-stabilized, and only the solar cells facing the Sun collect any power. In Fig 2 the paddle-mounted solar arrays leave the spacecraft body free for other equipment, and the paddles may have automatic controls so that they always face the Sun. Fig 3, the oriented panel system, shows a spacecraft which has to keep its antennas and other sensors pointed very precisely at whatever it is studying; usually this also has a Sun-tracking system which automatically moves the solar panel so that it always faces the Sun.

CHAPTER NINE

LOOKING FOR OTHER MANNED WORLDS

Section 45   Are They Really There?

The possibility that there may be other civilizations on planets in our own Milky Way Galaxy, and in the countless other Galaxies, was mentioned in Chapters 3 and 6. In fact many space scientists are now convinced that there *must* be advanced life forms in millions of other places in the Universe; and NASA is carrying out a seven-year search for such life. The project is called SETI—the Search for Extraterrestrial Intelligence—and a special team has been set up at NASA's Ames Research Center in California. Two years of preparation were due to be completed in 1979, with a five-year survey starting in 1980.

Why are we so sure that there are other worlds with people like us, when we have failed to find life anywhere else in our own Solar System? Only 30 years ago many people still thought there were 'canals' on Mars, and that we would find advanced life-forms there. By the time NASA's two Viking spacecraft landed in 1976, we already knew that was not so; there were, however, high hopes that their robot laboratories, analysing soil samples, would detect that there either were or had been at least some bacteria or other primitive life. Alas, the results were puzzling; it was impossible to be certain one way or the other. And it must be remembered that even though the landing sites were 7400 km apart, if two UFOs landed in the Sahara Desert and in the Antarctic, they might have ended just as uncertain about the possibilities of life on Earth.

Probably few people would have got very excited if the Viking spacecraft had found a few primitive fleas or worms in the Martian soil; but just think what it would really mean. It would prove beyond all doubt that on any planet or other body in the Universe where temperatures and other conditions were somewhat similar to those on Earth, life would begin to develop just as it has done here.

So how many places are there in the Universe where conditions are somewhat similar to those on Earth? In our own tiny Solar System, we

NASA has now launched three HEAOs (High Energy Astronomy Observatories), and they are making new discoveries about the Universe and its Black Holes, Pulsars, Neutron Stars etc. They are not only scanning the Milky Way Galaxy (top left) which contains our own Solar System, but have already studied Quasars which are 15.5 thousand million light years from Earth. If they can find Quasars 18–20 thousand million light years away they will be looking back to the point at which they believe the Universe was created

know for certain that there is no life as advanced as our own; we may still find *some* form of life on Mars; and one or two of the moons of Jupiter and Saturn (Callisto in the case of Jupiter; Titan in the case of Saturn) may have suitable conditions for life forms. But if there were any men on these bodies, with advanced technologies sending out radio waves, we would certainly have detected them by now.

But of course our own Solar System is only a tiny part of the Milky Way Galaxy—that creamy river of stars you can see across the sky on a clear, moonless night. NASA's SETI team points out that our Milky Way Galaxy probably contains about 300,000 million stars. (There are about

10,000 million other galaxies, each with just as many or more stars, but it is best not to think about them for the moment!) Among those 300,000 million stars, our own Sun is just one very common type of star. So Professor Carl Sagan, the famous astronomer who is a member of the SETI team, thinks it reasonable to assume that there are about one million places in our own galaxy where there are 'technical civilizations' *more advanced* than our own. That may seem a lot; in fact Carl Sagan's arithmetic suggests that only one star in 250,000 has a planet or moon capable of supporting life. And since our own Sun has at least 43 planets and moons, it merely suggests that, throughout the rest of our galaxy, one body in 7 million could be somewhat similar to Earth. That, surely, is not at all unlikely!

Section 46 How to Find Them

Having decided that there must be other people in other worlds, the next problem is how to locate them. Until recently, as Professor Sagan points out, we could not even start to look. Now, with radio astronomy, we have the tools. Civilizations more advanced than ours, we can assume, will already have discovered radio astronomy. That being so, some of our nearest neighbours may quite recently have discovered *our* existence.

The reason for that is quite simple. For the last 25 years or so we have been quite unintentionally 'announcing' our existence by all the radio and radar signals spreading out from Earth into space at the speed of light. For anyone with the equipment to pick up these signals and the knowledge to recognize them, evidence of our existence—and *of our exact state of development* is spreading out at the rate of 300,000 km per second, or over 1000M kph.

The total distance that light (and a radio wave) travels in a year is known as 'one light year'—a very useful unit when talking or writing about the Universe's astronomical distances. The nearest star to us is 4.3 light years away; Sirius, the brightest star in our sky, is 8.7 light years away. Barnard's Star, six light years away, is believed to have two or more planets, and the British Interplanetary Society recently worked out a project to launch the unmanned 'Starship Daedalus' towards it at a mere 135M kph. Even at that speed however, it would be a 50-year journey. But such distances are not impossible if we merely want to start up radio conversations. There are about 150 stars which might have planets like our own within 50 light years of Earth; so if they each averaged 40 planets

The Arecibo Observatory in Puerto Rico. Only a small part of its observation time is spent searching for life on other worlds

and moons, we immediately have 6000 possible bodies on which to look for possible neighbours.

Not that astronomers always think the nearest stars are the best places to look. In November 1974, at a ceremony to mark the resurfacing of the world's largest radio/radar telescope at Arecibo, a signal was sent to a cluster of a million stars called M13 which happened to be overhead. The message will take 24,000 light years to get there—enough time for a civilization to develop on one of their planets before it gets there; enough time too for that civilization to die, or destroy itself, before their reply arrives back here in 48,000 years from now!

Since 1960 at least nine attempts have been made by observatories in both America and Russia to detect signals of 'extraterrestrial intelligent origin'—in other words, the sort of signals men would send out. All have failed. But it must be pointed out that it has been possible to study only a few targets—sometimes, say, a dozen nearby sunlike stars, or pulsed signals from the entire sky. About 1000 individual stars have been examined, but mostly for such short periods that there was no real chance that our instruments were tuned in to them at the exact time needed to receive signals they would have sent out many years ago.

Some Soviet scientists think we may already be hearing the broadcast activities of 'super-civilizations' and assuming that they are natural noises. Quasars, mysterious points of light which send out far more energy and radio waves than an entire galaxy, could in fact be super-civilizations, according to Russia's Dr Nikolai Kardashov. Since the first quasar was discovered in 1963, over 200 have been found. Perhaps the noises we hear are these quasar civilizations communicating with one another.

In the last few years, by linking the latest radio telescopes to the latest computers, it has become possible for the first time to make a real search among the baffling maze of noises that bombard Earth from outer space. Most of these are the 'natural' noises radiated by the Sun's constant thermo-nuclear explosions, storms on Jupiter, the explosion and formation of new stars. Now NASA's SETI team is planning to use the huge 26 and 9m antennas of the Deep Space Network at Goldstone, California, to try to sort out the muddle of noise. Eighty per cent of the sky will be surveyed, and the signals divided into 1 million separate channels. Ironically, the search for other men in other worlds will be carried out for us by robots, because they can do it much quicker and more cheaply than human brains. They can also gather other useful information at the same time.

Later plans are to continue the search with space telescopes, and from bases on the farside of the Moon, where there will be less interference from our domestic television and radar transmissions.

Section 47   *Is It Safe to Speak to Strange Worlds?*

Some scientists and politicians think we should just listen, and not attempt to make contact with other civilizations, until we can be sure that they are friendly. But the only civilizations we shall be able to contact seem certain to be more advanced than we are, or contact would not be possible. The most important and urgent thing for us to learn is whether other civilizations have found ways of living in peace and harmony with each other, and then of surviving when the resources of their original planets have all been used, as may happen with Earth in a few centuries' time. It may be that other civilizations, able to observe us before we can contact them, have already decided we are not worth bothering with until we have made more progress on our own. So, as in every human activity, what is likely to pay off in the long run is not Caution, but Courage.

A POSTSCRIPT ABOUT THE UNIVERSE

As a sort of postscript I thought I should add the latest names given by astronomers to different sorts of stars with notes on how they seem to behave, provided by NASA. Like everything else, it seems, stars are born and finally die—though their lifetime lasts billions of years. And the way they end apparently differs according to their size. There is no need to worry if you find it hard to understand when a Supernova becomes a Black Hole, or a Red Giant becomes a Black Dwarf. These names just describe ideas and theories about what *may* be going on in the Universe. Nobody yet knows all the facts: though at last we do seem to be moving towards the time when we shall fully understand how the Universe in which we live really works. Then we shall truly have reached the SPACE AGE.

Supernova   A massive star which finally ends its life with a violent explosion. Its remaining material is hurled about the Universe, to mix with what scientists call 'the primeval hydrogen'. From this mixture new stars are later formed. Our Sun, for instance, is believed to have been formed from the debris of countless other stars which exploded before it was born. Supernovas, or massive star explosions, are believed to result in Neutron Stars and Black Holes; smaller stars, like our Sun, are believed to become White Dwarfs (see page 125).

Pulsars and Neutron Stars   Only discovered in 1967, Pulsars emit radio signals whose pulsations are extremely precise. Some people think the signals might be sent out by advanced civilizations; but the evidence suggests that Pulsars are fast-spinning neutron stars. That means bodies of densely packed neutrons (atomic particles having no electric charge), which are believed to form when a large star burns up its fuel and collapses. A whole star might become a tight ball only 15 km in diameter, so closely packed that a spoonful of material from the centre would weigh 1000M tonnes. A Neutron Star, or Pulsar, has been located in the centre of the Crab Nebula, a glowing cloud which is still expanding from a Supernova reported by the Chinese in 1054

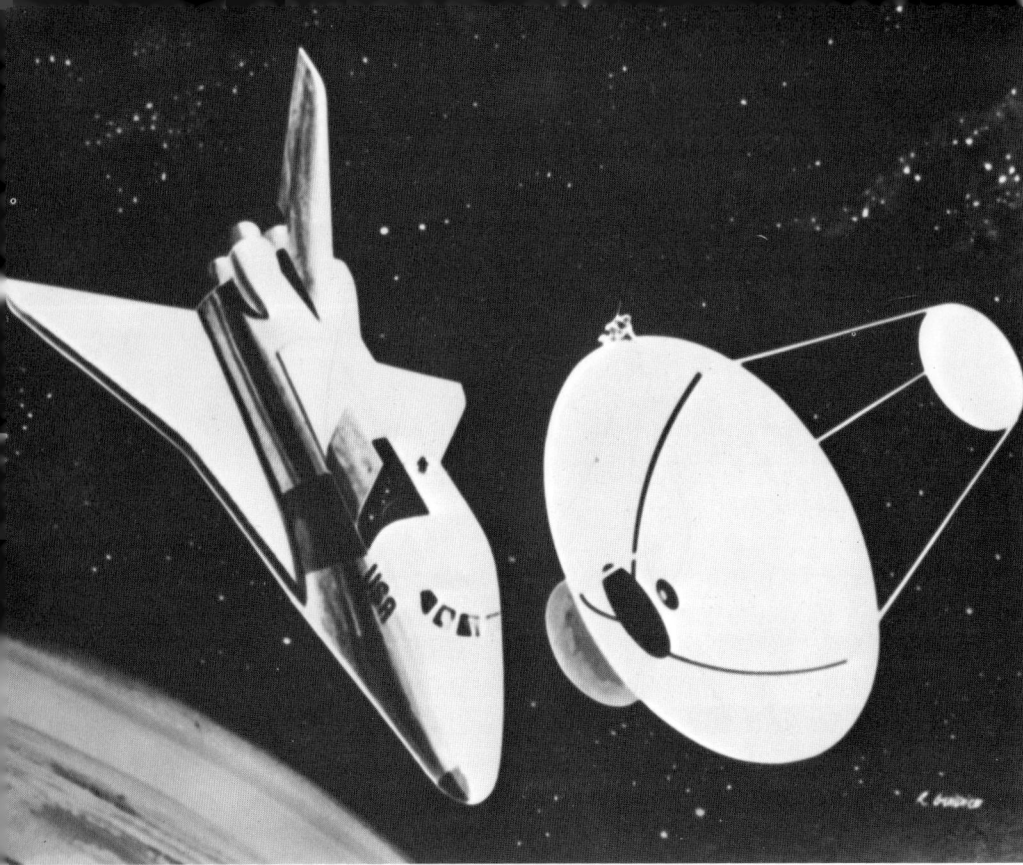

Black Holes   Believed to be the final stage in the collapse of a dying star which was very massive. Even more densely packed than a Neutron Star, its gravitational force is so great that even light waves are unable to escape. Since Black Holes emit no light or other radiation, their existence cannot be confirmed by direct observation, but is predicted by the laws of relativity. Cygnus X-1, a powerful X-ray source in the constellation Cygnus, is believed to be a Black Hole, rotating with a visible star around a common centre of gravity. It is believed to be drawing material from the visible star—really 'eating' its companion. The space writer Adrian Berry believes that Black Holes have hollow, rotating centres, and that a carefully piloted spaceship could pass through the centre to arrive instantly in a different part of the Universe, thus conquering the problem of having to travel at the speed of light for many years to reach other stars and their planets. But the spaceship would have to match its speed to that of the rotating hole at *643M kph*, and enter the navigable centre of the Black Hole which is only 585 m in diameter! And because there is no convenient Black Hole near Earth, Mr Berry has written a book, *The Iron Sun*, explaining exactly how we can make our own Black Hole just one light year from Earth.

Red Giant An old star approaching the end of its life. Having burnt the hydrogen at its core, it starts to burn the hydrogen in its outer layers which makes it turn red and swell to 100 times its previous size. If it is a small star it then contracts and becomes a White Dwarf; if it is a large star it becomes a Supernova and explodes.

White Dwarf A small aging star in its last stages. Having burnt all its hydrogen, it cannot generate enough pressure at its centre to balance the crushing force of gravity, and collapses under its own weight. White Dwarfs contract to about the size of Earth, then spend many years gradually losing their heat. Eventually the White Dwarf burns out completely, leaving a Black Dwarf.

Quasars Astronomers believe Quasars may be the most remote objects in the Universe, and are baffled by them. They look like stars when seen through an optical telescope, but send out more energy at radio frequencies than whole galaxies. Could these possibly be civilizations?

America's Pioneer 10 and 11 spacecraft, now leaving the Solar System after exploring Jupiter and Saturn, both carry this plaque. Drawings of men and women, shown in relation to the size of the craft, and symbols showing where it came from in the Solar System, might in millions of years be seen by intelligent creatures in other worlds

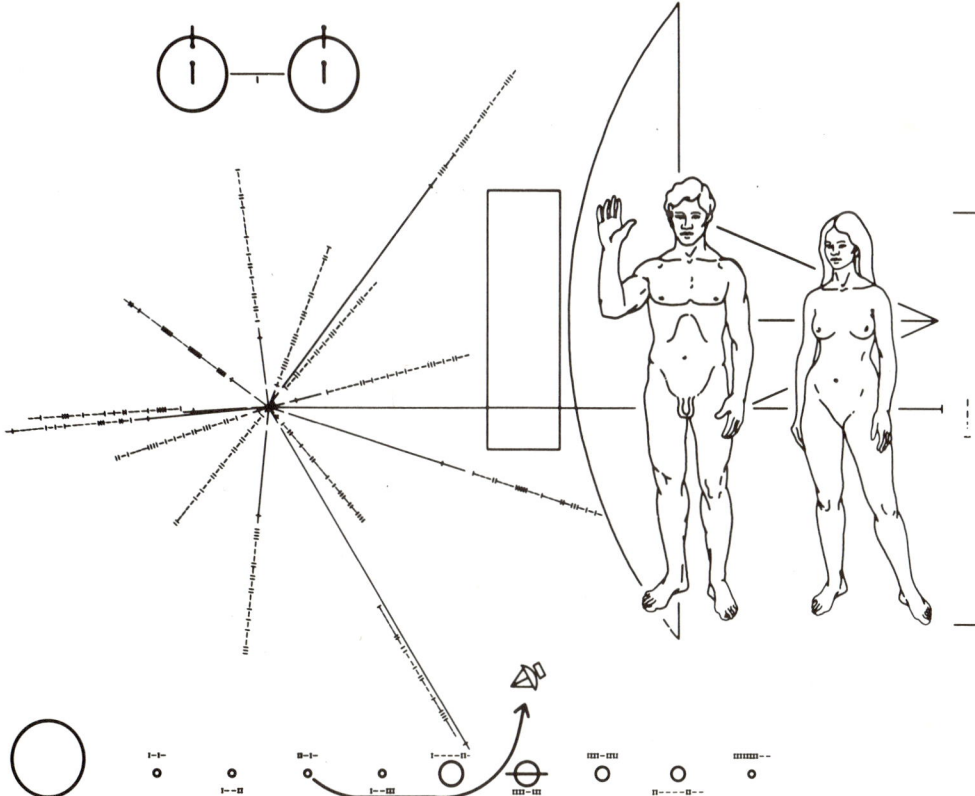

INDEX